7. April 1974.   May this inspire
you to float your way over here !
        Tom & Jan

D1187168

LA
BALSA
TO
AUSTRALIA

LA BALSA TO AUSTRALIA

THE LONGEST RAFT VOYAGE IN HISTORY

BY VITAL ALSAR
WITH ENRIQUE HANK LOPEZ

HODDER AND STOUGHTON
LONDON SYDNEY AUCKLAND TORONTO

A mi familia
Y a La Liga Navál de España

"Within the four seas all men are brothers. . . ."

Confucius
5th Century B.C.

LA
BALSA
TO
AUSTRALIA

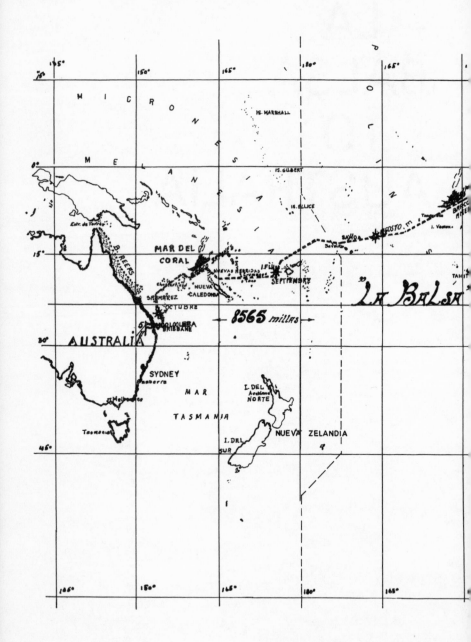

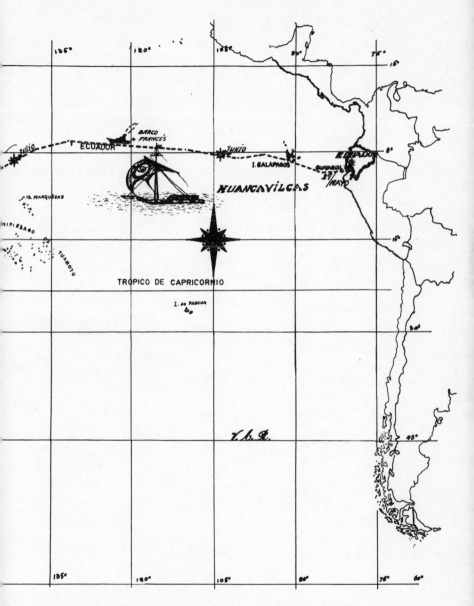

Route of *La Balsa* from Ecuador to Australia, drawn by Vital Alsar

PROLOGUE

On our ninety-seventh day at sea, a violent storm almost destroyed our wooden raft. Watching my three crew members stubbornly holding onto the mast, which was on the verge of collapsing in the howling gale, I suddenly remembered a conversation between my father and mother.

"This boy will be eaten by sharks someday," my father prophesied. "He's always fooling around the ocean."

"I guess Vital loves the sea," replied my mother.

"That's not love," he grumbled. "It's madness. He's going to be a sailor—and all sailors are crazy."

"What about Columbus?" she asked, a hint of defiance in her usually soft voice.

"He was crazy too," my father answered with implacable conviction. "No one else was foolhardy enough to try to reach the east by sailing west. By all rational standards, he was obviously insane."

Perhaps my father was right. If indeed all men who take to the sea are touched with madness, this book is a perfect case history of their affliction. It is the story of four men who built a balsa wood raft and sailed it across the Pacific from South America to Australia—8,600 miles in six months' time —the longest raft voyage in all recorded history.

1

We began our journey on one of those dark moonless nights that my superstitious grandmother would have called a "bad time for starting anything."

Two hours past midnight on May 29, 1970, as the tidal currents of the brackish Río Guayas began to ebb, a small dumpy tugboat edged carefully toward the dock to take *La Balsa* under tow. We had hoped to make the first stage of our journey from Guayaquil, Ecuador, under sail. But after having watched the river's unpredictable currents, and having read the warnings printed in vivid purple letters on the navigation charts—"channel buoys are unreliable and may be extinguished, missing, or out of position"—we had sought the help of a tugboat captain with plenty of local knowledge to guide us out to sea.

Even so, the 120-mile journey down the river and across the turbulent Gulf of Guayaquil would take a long time, almost three days, since we could be towed only at very low speed. And from the moment the line on our bow snapped taut, the raft seemed to hold back, like a fighting bull clinging to its *querencia,* that special area of the bull ring where it feels protected from the matador.

"The raft must know something we don't," said Gabriel. "It senses danger out there."

"No, it just doesn't like being towed," I replied. "Rafts like to flow with the winds and the currents and they show how unhappy they are in these conditions. Anyway, we'll reach the ocean safely. That's where the real enemy is."

I should have said "enemies." There would be many lying in wait for us, some we couldn't even anticipate. But we did know that the equatorial climate of the Pacific would be blisteringly hot and chillingly cold, that there were untold numbers of treacherous reefs, that sharks would be trailing us almost daily, that we might fight among ourselves, that we might be crushed by a ship on a fog-shrouded night, that we could starve or die of thirst.

All these possibilities flitted through our minds, but we never spoke of them. And the next morning, when the sun rose behind us, revealing the tropical beauty of the South American coast, there was only optimism on board. The Gulf of Guayaquil was more beautiful than we expected, with palm-fringed beaches and coves and densely foliaged hills that curved away to the southwest.

"They've been good to us," reflected Marc, as he watched the shoreline recede. "Those Ecuadorians are a fine people."

We had little time for such reminiscences; the water was

rougher than we had expected. In the feverish excitement of the previous night, I had been almost totally unaware of the raft's motion. My attention was focused on other matters— the last-minute stashing away of camera, film, maps and navigational tools with the aid of a pocket flashlight in the pitch-black night, checking the caps on gasoline cans, testing the centerboard *guaras*. Now I suddenly became aware of the jerky, lurching movements of the raft—and the periodic splashing of the waves across the bow.

My stomach felt it first, a faint queasiness that gradually churned down into my belly like serpents moiling inside me and then rushing to my throat. I staggered back to the stern and started to vomit before I reached the edge. When I told Marc about the snakes in my gut, he laughed and told me to go and lie down.

The following day, however, Marc and Gabriel were also sick. "I've got your snakes, Vital," said Gabriel with a groan. A few hours later Normand joined the sick squad, and since we were all suffering from varying degrees of nausea, I felt less embarrassed about my own condition.

The constant seesawing of the raft seemed particularly acute when we huddled inside the cabin in the evening. But we tried to take our minds off our discomfort by playing poker under a swaying lantern hanging from the low ceiling. In the pale, quivering light, I studied my three companions.

Marc Modena, aged forty-four, was the oldest. A weatherbeaten man with a gentle sense of humor, we sometimes called him *Pepere* (Grandpa). His long angular nose and firm mouth appeared to be carved from granite, and his scraggly beard concealed a strong chin. Marc had sailed with me on the ill-fated raft, *Pacifica,* which sank near the Galapagos Islands in 1966, nearly costing us our lives. Thereafter he returned to his wife and two daughters in Montreal, where he was manager of a large restaurant, Le Gobelet. He was the ideal principal chef and supply master. He was also an experienced sailor. For five years he had been a signaler in the French Navy, and in 1956 he was on the crew of *Egare II,* a red cedar raft that crossed the Atlantic from Nova Scotia to England.

Our youngest crew member was Normand Tetreault, twenty-six years old and a Canadian. Because of his quiet, taciturn manner and his thick bushy hair and beard, we called him *L'Homme du Bois* (Man of the Woods). Always quick to smile although he was quiet and shy, he was convinced that most conversation was an intolerable chore. Thus he frequently had only one response to anything that was said: "Oh boy." That, and nothing more. This was extremely disconcerting at first, but we soon realized that he could say "Oh boy" in so many different ways that it became an entirely new two-word language. An industrial designer with a lifelong love of sailing, Normand had built his own oceangoing sloop and was taking a course in celestial navigation when Marc asked him to join us. "He's also an amateur parachutist," Marc later informed me. "But I don't think that will help him much on *La Balsa.*"

The pessimist of our crew was Gabriel Salas, a twenty-seven-year-old Chilean who had studied geology for five years at the University of Chile. Full of charm and quick intelligence, he had blue-gray eyes that brimmed with mischief. Since he was half German, Gabriel was fairer than the rest of us, even with a solid wind-chafed tan. He had been hitchhiking around South America for several months and happened to arrive in Guayaquil as we began building our raft. With no thought of compensation, he immediately volunteered to help us, working as hard as anyone else. I knew, without his having to tell me, that he wanted to sail with us. But I thought he might be too much of a hippie—too unstable for the long haul. He wrote poetry in his spare time and frequently talked about political revolutions. On the other hand, he could be extremely logical, pragmatic, and disturbingly skeptical. I had reserved judgment on him, hoping to find out how serious he was and if he could adapt himself to the rest of us.

Even after deciding to take him along, I held him off, feigning indifference when he told me he was shipping out on a freighter. Then, as we were standing on the pier to wish him goodbye, I shouted, "Will you come with us, Gabriel?" Without a moment's hesitation, he scrambled off the ship with a wild "YIPPIE!" On our way back to *La Balsa,* he reached into the watch pocket of his trousers and took out a gold coin worth fifty dollars. "Take this," he said. "I know the rest of you have contributed a lot more, but this is all I have."

Curiously enough, all four of us were about the same height and weight—around five feet ten or eleven inches and roughly 160 to 170 pounds. Consequently, it was easy to sleep in equally divided spaces inside our small cabin, seldom touching each other except when a particularly strong jolt tipped the raft from side to side. But it was not the lurching that bothered us most. It was the tedium of our jerky pace, and it made me wonder how (or if) we could possibly cover 8,600 miles in less than a year. Gabriel, always the skeptic, openly expressed his doubts.

"Are you really sure we'll make it in five or six months?" he asked.

"We'll go much faster on the open sea," I said.

Marc nodded in agreement—nothing could discourage him—and Normand mumbled an "Ooh boy" that was a mixture of doubt and resignation.

We had pulled out of Guayaquil with fifty-two gallons of water and seventeen gallons of gasoline stored under the floor of the cabin. The gasoline was for a 115-volt electric generator that would run our radio, which was stored in one corner of the woven cane cabin in eight plastic bags to protect it from the waves that would periodically pour through the cabin window and open doorway. There were also two hammocks and four sleeping bags stuffed into the cabin, which was twelve feet long, seven feet wide, and only four and a half feet at its highest point in the middle.

Our food stores were kept in or under the cabin in a wooden box perched on the logs near the stern. We had 330 pounds of canned fruit, 220 pounds of potatoes, 44 pounds of flour, 44 pounds of rice, 44 pounds of dried beans, 220 pounds of green bananas, and 220 pounds of unripened oranges.

"If we're lucky," Marc said when we teased him about his apparent fetish for even numbers, "we'll have enough for half the trip. We'll probably lose a good twenty percent of this through rot or water damage."

Our native forerunners, the Huancavilca Indians of Ecuador (lesser known than the Incas of Peru but just as advanced in many respects during the fifteenth and sixteenth centuries) had eaten a species of potato called *kumara,* but we had been unable to find any in Guayaquil. They had also eaten dried meat and fish, which were not available in any of the markets we visited. Instead we expected to catch fish every day as our staple diet and, true to expectations, we had sixty days of fresh fish during our first seventy-two days at sea.

The ocean would be both friend and foe, benign and aggressive from one minute to the next. During the towing, however, it seemed totally malignant. The coastal waters crashed against the raft, making it lurch and reel like a wooden drunkard, and most of us were still seasick and miserable at the end of the second day. At least we could take some comfort in the knowledge that our progress would be smoother when we reached the open sea. As we approached that vast expanse, however, Gabriel was visibly worried. Though he was willing to try anything, he couldn't mask his natural skepticism about whether we could actually sail twice as far as Thor Heyerdahl's legendary *Kon-Tiki*. Although Heyerdahl's earlier voyage had proved the seaworthiness of balsa rafts built according to ancient Indian designs, there were still many critics who thought we would fail. For, after all, we were planning to go twice as far as the *Kon-Tiki* and, beyond the Tahitian island where Heyerdahl finally pulled ashore with his water-logged raft, we would face 4,300 additional miles of some of the most treacherous seas in the world. Huge coral reefs, often hundreds of miles long, would be blocking our path like jagged petrified monsters half-submerged in a perpetual spray of angry waves.

Admiral Samuel Fernandez of the Mexican Navy had given me detailed charts pinpointing most of the barrier reefs in the South Seas, but he had cautioned me against complete reliance on them.

"Many reefs, even some large ones, haven't been charted yet," he had warned me. "And thousands of small ones are lying just below the surface. Unseen traps that never get on a map."

Night after night for several months, hunched over the maps spread across my kitchen table in Mexico City, I had studied and memorized hundreds of dots, lines, and shaded areas that represented dangerous reefs, tricky currents as strong as rivers, and seasonal weather changes. The vast stretch of water between Samoa and Australia would be especially hazardous for craft without radar. Night sailing, particularly on moonless nights, would be as chancy as Russian roulette. Hundreds of vessels, large and small, had been torn apart in this region.

"You're crazy, Vital!" exclaimed an old Mexican friend when I showed him my maps. "How can you possibly avoid those reefs without a motor or radar?"

"That's why I'm going," I said. "To prove that a simple raft can be navigated on the most treacherous seas. All the way across the Pacific."

"I still think you're mad," he said, looking at the projected route I'd outlined in dark ink.

Such gloomy comments might have discouraged most people, but my crew and I had become impervious to gloom. We had been hearing negative forecasts for months, many of them from old and trusted friends who spoke from long experience. "Mira, amigo," one of them told me, "the devil knows more because he's old than because he's the devil." And he had advised us to abandon the trip.

Marc would smile when he heard such talk. "These poor fools," he once said. "They think we'll be persuaded with reason. They don't realize that for a madman two and two do not equal four—that we have our own special logic."

There was, however, considerable method in what we were doing. I had spent countless days and nights in the naval archives and libraries of Mexico, Ecuador, and Peru, studying the amazing navigation techniques of the pre-Columbian Indians. Pouring through time-yellowed documents in Ecuador, I copied meticulously detailed sketches of balsa rafts which the Huancavilca Indians had sailed before the

Spaniards arrived in the New World. The first record of these rafts dates back to the early sixteenth century, when Captain Bartolomé Ruiz, one of Pizarro's most skilled navigators, spotted a raft filled with fruit and dried fish sailing far out on the Pacific between Guayaquil and the port of Lima. In a subsequent report to the King of Spain he said that the Indians had developed safer and better ways of sailing the coastal waters of South America than anything he had seen in Europe. He particularly mentioned the special keel boards, or *guaras,* which gave the Huancavilcas such control of their balsa rafts that they actually maneuvered more effectively than the traditional Spanish galleons.

In his writings, Juan Moricz, a distinguished Argentine anthropologist and keen student of pre-Columbian tribal migrations, offers strong evidence of long voyages across the Pacific in these ancient rafts. He points out that the Huancavilcas thought of the ocean as "a forest of rivers," with predictable currents to and from the Polynesian islands. They also knew about "friendly and unfriendly" winds and the use of astronomy in navigation. Commenting on the presence of South American cocoa trees, *quecha kuka,* in the far-off Mexican highlands, Moricz concludes that the Ecuadorian natives had sailed all the way to Mexico long before the conquest of Montezuma by Hernán Cortés.

Perhaps our friends would have been less skeptical had they known of Moricz and his theories, but I'm sure my wife's parents would have been unimpressed. My father-in-law, who, like my wife, is a classic Spanish dancer, worried about the gales and hurricanes that would surely wash us overboard "and splinter that little raft into a thousand pieces." To emphasize the point he would gyrate his hands like two hurricanes colliding in midair.

My wife, Denise, probably agreed with him. How else

should a woman feel when her husband leaves the family to risk his life on a fool's errand? The sea, my grandmother once told me, is a hard mistress for a sailor's wife to compete against. I imagine Denise would say "aye" to that. Yet she never tried to dissuade me. There were moments, nevertheless, when I detected a hint of doubt in her eyes, a fleeting nuance of skepticism in her inquiries about my plans. But no overt objections—at least, not in my presence.

Sometimes her mother would try to provoke an objection, asking such questions as: "Why must Vital desert his two children? Has he no concern for them? Doesn't he love you?" And Denise would simply shrug her shoulders, answering in a soft firm voice, "We'll be all right, Mother. You simply don't understand Vital. He has to do this. He's got to prove whatever he's got to prove, and he won't rest until he does. Nor will I. So please don't interfere." But in spite of her moral support, I knew that she was worried, that the prospect of becoming a young widow was never far from her mind.

Preoccupied by thoughts of my family, I hardly noticed the subtle changes in my own surroundings. The Bay of Guayaquil had been steadily receding, and the water had turned from a murky brown to a clear bright green. On the horizon the Pacific stretched before us.

"We're here!" yelled Gabriel, cupping a handful of water and splashing it on his face. With a ceremonial blast of its foghorn, the towboat cast us adrift on the open sea. We felt a mixture of optimism and awe. We were alone now on this giant body of water that would feed us, wash us, carry us toward our goal—or perhaps kill us at any moment.

Our awe suddenly gave way to a surge of joy, as we began dousing our faces with the cold salt water. In our en-

thusiasm, we almost forgot to thank the captain of the tugboat. He had cast off the heavy manila towline at his end,
yelling that he was donating it to *La Balsa* as he circled
around us before heading back to port. The tugboat had a
white superstructure and a black hull and bore the name
Guayaipe.

"What does that mean?" asked Marc.

"I don't know," I said. "It's probably an Indian name.
It certainly doesn't sound Spanish."

"I think it means *goodbye forever*," suggested Gabriel
with a mock frown. "The captain probably knows something he's not telling us."

"Maybe it's the sharks," said Marc.

"What sharks?" asked Gabriel, his eyes widening.

"The ones behind you," answered Marc, pointing to a
couple of dorsal fins slicing through the water about twenty
feet behind us.

"My god!" said Gabirel. *"Qué monstruos!* They must
be ten feet long."

"You'd better get used to them," I said. "They'll be
with us all the way."

2

Freed of the towline, our little raft floated with remarkable ease, and I was thankful for the many hours of work we had put into her construction. We had resolved to find seven "most female" logs for the raft—light, hollow balsa trees that would resound with a prolonged *thooongg* when slapped with the heel of the hand. The Ecuadorian Indians, following the precepts of their ancient ancestors, had advised us never to cut down a balsa tree until there was a crescent moon, when the sap has drained from the trunk. Such sap-drained trees are called "female," while the heavier sap-filled logs are "male." So we had waited patiently for a waning moon to cut the trees at their most female stage.

Our logging expedition began in Quito, the capital of Ecuador. Perched on a high Andean plateau, more than

9,300 feet above sea level, the city offers a splendid vista of snow-capped mountains whose slopes drop abruptly into dark green jungles and tropical rivers. The sky is a clear, vivid blue, unsullied by the smog and pollution of most urban centers. . Walking along the winding cobblestone streets, I was intrigued by the contrasts of the city's architecture. Founded by the Spaniard Sebastian de Benalcazar in 1534, Quito is a charming blend of simple whitewashed houses and exotic Spanish-Moorish estates and government buildings. The people—some 500,000 inhabitants—possess a spontaneous generosity and quiet dignity that won our hearts. Wherever we went, we were welcomed warmly.

Shortly after our arrival, we were invited to the National Palace to meet José María Velasco-Ibarra, the President of Ecuador, a man of advancing years but young in energy and spirit. He wished us success on our voyage and offered to help us in any way he could.

"Men like you make history," he said. "With courage— and luck—you will revive this ancient art of balsa raft navigation. Go with God and the benediction of our country."

We thanked him and left to continue preparations for our expedition. His words had given us new inspiration.

It was a bright cool morning when we left Quito, crowded into a tightly packed Land Rover. Later we switched to a couple of jeeps and finally left the jeeps in a small village when the dirt roads became too narrow for automotive transport. From there we proceeded on foot, with all our camping and woodcutting gear perched on the backs of three sturdy mules.

As we made our way slowly down the mountainside, I was dazzled by the dramatic landscape. The western slope of the Andean range dipped abruptly to the jungle far below, with occasional paths cut along narrow shelves of loose rock that teetered on the edge of deep gorges. Progressing single file along the nearly perpendicular paths and winding precipices, we looked down menacing cliffs and hugged the walls for safety. Then, as we got lower, ultimately descending some ten thousand feet, the paths were wider and a bit more level, allowing us to travel with greater ease and confidence.

"It's safer—but hotter," said Marc, unbuttoning his shirt.

The air grew warmer and damper with each downward loop of the road, with clouds of vapor rising through narrow gorges and often obscuring the green bluffs and ridges just ahead of us. It was like walking into a hothouse, the stifling air deadened with an excess of perfume. It reminded me of a funeral I'd been forced to attend as a child when one of the rich old *influyentes* of our seaside town died.

The air was even heavier as we neared the jungle floor, with its gurgling muddy streams. Soft clay banks, lush with various shades of moss, yielded a bewildering array of ferns and giant plants with leaves like elephant ears. Swarms of insects crawled through the foliage or spun in the vaporous air like jittery grains of black pepper. Lizards and snakes slithered in and out, vibrating the leaves behind them.

"We know where they've *been*," said Marc, pulling back a still-trembling rubber leaf. "But not where they are."

Jaguars, iguanas, larger reptiles, and other jungle residents were also lurking nearby. This we knew from their sounds, and from the conversation of our guides, but we could see very few of them. The birds, however, were highly visible in their brilliant plumage—and incredibly vocal.

"They apparently don't like Spaniards and Frenchmen," said Don Cesar Iglesias, our lumber expert. "I've never heard them act like this before."

"These mosquitos are worse," I said, brushing aside a horde that surrounded me like a halo. "They're racist." (While I consider myself free of ethnic paranoia, I was sure none of our native guides were bitten.) The mosquitos and gnats were bad, but we worried even more about poisonous snakes, scorpions, giant ants, and tarantulas. On our second day in the jungle, close to the balsa forest, I foolishly whacked an innocent-looking bamboo trunk with my machete, and a covey of giant black ants sprang out. I pulled back my machete for a second slash when Don Cesar caught my arm and yanked me away from the bamboo.

"They'll kill you!" he yelled. "They're almost as poisonous as snakes!" When we were safely away, he told me it would be a quick but painful death. There was no way to counteract their venom.

One of our woodcutters had an even closer brush. He had just cut down a dead tree and stepped back to see it fall, when he heard a hiss and felt something snap at his loose pantsleg. Turning around, he saw a long slithery black snake, whose tail was pinioned by the fallen trunk.

"You're lucky he was trapped by that tree, *amigo*," said Don Cesar. Then carefully circling behind the still menacing snake, he neatly severed its head with a deft slash of his machete.

As for the scorpions, we were advised that they were not necessarily deadly, but always painful. Since they preferred nighttime activity, we were cautioned to keep our mosquito nets tightly tucked around our cots and to shake out our shoes and clothes before dressing. We took the same precautions against tarantulas, which sometimes haunted my dreams.

Lying there in the menacing jungle darkness, I longed for the great open vistas of the Pacific where the dangers were of a more familiar kind and dimension. Even before the faint gray trace of dawn appeared through the overhanging foliage, I was anxious to get on with the logging. For a moment I debated whether to wake my crewmates, who were snoring like soft lazy thunder. Then, convincing myself that too much sleep would debilitate them, I cupped my hands and, imitating a bugle, sounded reveille with all my might. Within minutes they were crawling out of their cots and palm leaf *petates,* mumbling ugly things about Pizarro and all the lousy Spaniards that followed him.

As we had moved deeper into the jungle I noticed that fewer and fewer people we met spoke Spanish, their soft nasal voices uttering native dialects I'd never heard. Their poor scrimpy straw huts clung to the mountains like mushrooms, their goats and other animals lazily grazing nearby.

Leaving the last of these outposts behind, we had trudged on through the lush mountain foliage. Then, as we neared a valley stream, we came upon an isolated bamboo hut, with a woman grinding meal in a stone mortar and several children splashing in the water nearby.

"How can they survive so far from civilization?" Marc wondered openly.

"They're perfectly self-sufficient," I replied. "They have rich soil, fruits, game. What more do they need?"

As though to reinforce my argument, a man with a sunbaked face appeared, carrying a string of silver-gray fish. He beckoned us over, asked us to join them, and soon we were all seated around a sumptuous feast of rice, corn, bananas, pork, and fresh river fish broiled over a low fire. Our hosts were cheerful and animated, eager to know all about our expedition, which we explained with the help of our guides. We all agreed it was one of the finest meals we'd ever enjoyed—and one of the most civilized.

Bidding our new-found friends goodby, we continued on. Our guides, who were native to the region, could locate by what seemed like instinct the best balsa forests in Ecuador. Time and again, as we came upon a cluster of balsa, they would knock their knuckles against a tree trunk and listen carefully. If it wasn't the precise hollowness they expected, one of them would mumble a phrase to Don Cesar, and he, in turn, would translate.

"That trunk is too *macho*."

"*Macho?*" asked Normand.

Don Cesar turned and winked at me. "Your friend Vital knows all about the *machos* and *hembras*," he said.

The old man was referring to my previous experimentation with "male" and "female" balsa wood after our ill-fated *Pacifica* voyage. The logs of that raft had become so badly infected with fungus that they rotted away in mid-ocean and, to avoid another such disaster, I had decided to learn more about the properties of balsa. First, I had read all the literature I could find on the subject. Then I had gone to the Instituto Nacional de Silvicultura in Mexico City, where I had discussed the physical properties of all kinds of porous wood with experts. I learned, for example, that the sap in balsa trunks runs through tiny almost imperceptible channels between the larger pores of wood fiber. Thus, when the sap is full, it acts as a damper between the pores that produce the hollow sound when you strike the trunk—so when there's less sap there's more resonance between the pores.

I had also spent many hours studying the intricate internal structure of balsa with a high-powered microscope, probing the minute cells with sharp needles, and then floating numbered rectangular pieces of the wood in a tub of water to register the degree of buoyancy of each one. Consequently, when I first met Don Cesar just before our second expedition, I was crammed full of information about balsa. Undoubtedly annoyed by my arrogance, he decided to challenge me one night.

"Okay," he said, placing seven pieces of balsa wood on a table. "Let's see if you can tell me which of these are the best ones to use on a raft."

Weighing each one in my hand and examining the exposed ends I said, "This one's too *macho* . . . this is in between . . . this is two-thirds female . . . this one *macho* . . . this a good female." Right down the line, with very little hesitation.

He was obviously thinking about that incident as we slogged through the jungle searching for trees, and finally, deep in the jungle, we found a cluster of the right gender. Although the female trees were lighter than the sap-filled *machos,* the log of each tree probably weighed about a ton. Watching our helpers tug and strain, hauling the huge trunks one by one to the river bank, I felt a certain anxiety as to how well they would float. In spite of all my experimentation there was always that nibble of doubt.

My anxiety vanished, however, as each successive log was dumped into the water with a great splash, and then quickly bobbed clear of the surface. Most logs from any species of tree will float, but balsas can be maneuvered almost like plastic ducks in a bathtub. With hardly any effort, we lined them up side by side and lashed them together with cords made from lianas that we unwound from nearby jungle trees. Then we loaded this temporary makeshift raft with bamboo and lianas for later use, happily noting that the balsas took the additional weight without losing a centimeter of their rise above water level. Even when several of us climbed aboard, the logs maintained their fifty-fifty equipoise.

Thus we were happy and confident as we shoved away from the river bank into the swirling current that would propel us toward our construction site at Guayaquil, some 125 miles downstream. Our woodcutters and several villagers stood on shore, waving at us and yelling *"buena suerte! buena suerte!"*

Leaving the shade of the thick foliage that formed solid green walls on either side of the river, we could feel the sudden onslaught of the late-morning sun, a pulsating heat that drew shimmering clouds of vapor off the water. Our native guides and oarsmen seemed to accept the heat with no sign of discomfort, but Marc and I crawled under a shelter of freshly cut banana leaves and tried to ignore the hothouse humidity.

"It's either a furnace or a teakettle," I said, rubbing the rivulets of sweat off my chest. We considered diving into the river to cool off, but a trio of small alligators cavorting near the left bank quickly changed our minds. Rounding the bend of the wide muddy river, we saw a giant iguana perched on the edge of a clay bank, its heavy-lidded eyes watching us with sun-induced torpor and indifference, and its spiked back arched like an evil weapon from the Middle Ages.

As we got farther downstream, the villages were larger and more numerous, the people involved in various activities. We saw hundreds of dug-out canoes expertly punted with long poles by dark-skinned men of mixed Indian, Negro, and Spanish ancestry. We also saw several small balsa rafts heaped high with green bananas and other fruits, no doubt intended for markets in the larger towns to the west.

Seeing the fruit and smelling the piquant odors of cooking meat in every village we passed, we were soon stirred out of our lethargy. Using a small fire that our oarsmen had made in a bowl of wet clay, we cooked some fish and eggs and quenched our thirst with coconut milk. Then we leaned back in our leafy shelter and watched the villagers tending their day's-end chores with a weary when-will-it-all-end doggedness that one sees in poor people all over the world.

The next afternoon, the current slowed and the river widened, and we could begin to make out the sun-bleached buildings of Guayaquil—humble makeshift shacks, tin-roofed warehouses, low-rise apartment and office buildings, church spires piercing the blue horizon. On reaching the port city, we began construction immediately. Holding our seven logs next to each other, we pivoted them around so as to find the closest "fit" between their various contours. Marc was in charge of this particular operation, and he handled the balsas with infinite care, slowly rotating one log and then another in a painstaking search for the best possible pairings.

"He's a born matchmaker," observed Normand.

"It will be a strange match," I said. "They're all females."

"And how will four *machos* like us sustain a life together for six months?" Marc interjected.

The question had always been there in the back of my mind, persistent as a nagging toothache. How do four men live together for six months, twenty-four hours a day, in a cramped floating prison cell? We had all heard of prisoners going "stir crazy," sometimes killing each other because of a tiny provocation. Other traits could prove equally troublesome. Obviously, we couldn't expect to find four perfectly stable individuals. But we might be lucky enough to get four men whose neuroses would complement each other. We needed introverts and extroverts, optimists and pessimists, romantics and realists, conservatives and liberals—a mixed bag of human strengths and weaknesses. Even after we began building the raft, however, I still had some lingering doubts. There were times when Gabriel seemed too frivolous, when Normand seemed too quiet and introspective. Would they irritate each other? Would they finally clash? No one could answer such questions in advance, yet we had to establish a *modus vivendi* that would minimize friction and perhaps prevent a fatal blowup on board. (Wasn't it Gide who said there is a potential murderer in all of us?) Consequently, on a cool breezy evening about a week after our arrival at Guayaquil, I broached the subject as casually as possible.

With a cold after-dinner beer in my hand, I leaned back in my chair and stared reflectively at a wide jagged crack on the ceiling of the Hosteria Madrid, a modest neighborhood restaurant where we normally ate after work. "I've been thinking we should have some guidelines," I said, shifting my gaze from the ceiling.

"Like the division of work?" asked Marc.

"Well, that's important, but not exactly what we have to think about."

"What else *is* there?" asked Gabriel, fingering the rim of his glass.

"Our relationship to each other. It's going to be a long

journey in very close quarters, and we're bound to get on each other's nerves from time to time." I hesitated, searching for the right words, words that would suggest rather than command. "First of all, we should never violate each other's personal space. We should never—under any circumstances —touch each other. No horseplay, no sparring, no wrestling. . . ."

"But why?" interrupted Gabriel, his eyes squinting. "If it's only playing around . . ."

"That's just the point," I replied. "Once you have violated another man's space, even in fun, it will be easier to touch him in anger. So we've got to imagine that each of us is surrounded by an invisible bubble of privacy that must never be shattered."

"Another thing," I continued, "we must never criticize each other. We all have certain habits, little personal quirks, that will annoy someone else."

Gabriel softly drummed on the table with his fingers. "And you think even a small criticism could blow up into a fight?"

"Precisely. When you start to complain about a man's eating habits or his snoring or the way he talks or anything else—it makes no difference that you're only joking— human nature dictates that he will end up hating you."

"You want us to become saints," said Mark.

"For about five months. When we get to Australia we can be humans again."

The following morning I was up early to check the progress on our raft. Marc had indeed performed the best possible marriage between the seven logs. The longest, a forty-two-foot trunk, was placed in the middle, with the six shorter ones on either side, their forward ends cut on a diagonal to form a pointed bow that would cut through the water more easily. We then bound them together with separate lengths of thick hemp rope, presoaked in water for twenty-four hours for added pliancy. With a series of two-over-and-one-back loops, carefully fitting the rope into shallow parallel grooves carved into the logs, the basic structure of the raft began to take form on the wooden scaffold. We had decided not to build it on the cement wharf because of the continuous accumulation of rotting debris, which might infect the delicate balsa with fungus. As a further precaution, Marc coated the underside of the logs with crude oil.

Now we were ready to start on the superstructure. Four heavy beams were laid across the base logs and firmly secured with one-inch hemp. Then a deck of split bamboo was placed across the beams, creating narrow storage spaces between the deck and logs. The deck itself was covered with mats of woven reeds.

It was slow, tedious work: hundreds of knots to be tied tightly, with great precision. Knowing that if only a few knots were carelessly tied our raft might rip apart in mid-ocean, I found myself rechecking some that Gabriel had tied near the starboard stern. Each one was perfect, neatly tucked into its designated groove and pulled tight as a drumhead.

A few hours later I noticed Gabriel slyly checking some knots Marc had tied, and then I saw Normand checking my knots! I couldn't hold back the laughter.

"We're all spies," I said. "No one trusts anyone."

Gabriel was no less vigilant when we started to build the cabin, checking everyone's handiwork as if he were a strawboss on a construction gang. We tolerated his watchful skepticism with amusement—and gratitude—as he retightened every knot that fastened the thick corner bamboo posts to the lighter canes which formed the framework of the roof.

"We've got to be especially careful with the roof," I said. "If it comes loose in a high wind it'll be like a second sail."

Thus we took special pains with the walls of woven bamboo reeds and the roof panels, which were made from bamboo slats and tough pliable banana leaves. In front of the cabin we erected a thirty-foot mast made of two poles of hard durable mangrove wood, weighing about 350 pounds apiece. They were situated one on either side of the raft and tied together at the top to form an inverted V. To keep this structure upright we secured it fore and aft with three thick hemp ropes at the point of the V, one tied to the tip of the bow and the others tied to each corner of the stern. Atop this was a small crow's nest and a flagpole, from which in good weather we would fly the Spanish colors.

The sail was a rectangular sheet of very heavy, strong number-six Spanish canvas, eighteen feet wide and twenty-one feet high, that we hemmed on all sides with heavy cord to minimize tearing. In a moment of whimsy, I decorated it with a huge bright-red sun, in the center of which I painted a sketch of *La Balsa* itself. There wasn't room for a spare sail, but if repairs were needed we had plenty of thick thread and four packages of needles. The top of the sail was lashed to a boom about six inches in diameter. This we could pivot to the right or left on a ring located at the top of the mast. So that it could swing free of the base of the triangular mast, the bottom of the sail was not attached to anything, but simply secured at the corners by two long ropes that could be tightened or loosened so as to trim the sail in the desired direction.

Perhaps the raft's most advantageous feature was its set of *guaras*. These were nine vertical keel boards, or centerboards, about an inch and a half thick, two feet wide, and six to eight feet long. They were made of a soft, pliant wood called *figueroa,* which grows plentifully in Ecuador; we had learned about it from the Ecuadorian fishermen, who use it themselves to steer their flat-bottomed balsa rafts along the rivers and coastal waters much as their ancient predecessors did. They showed us how the *guaras* should be used on *La Balsa*. By raising or lowering them only a few inches, we ought to keep our otherwise clumsy raft on a steady course —a nautical miracle!

Supplementing this practical knowledge with the written records of the ancient Huancavilca navigational techniques, we carefully worked out the best possible locations of the *guaras*—three in a V-shaped formation near the bow, two under the cabin, and four in a straight line aft the cabin. Situated between the logs, they protruded under the raft like multiple fins. Thus, if we wanted to steer the raft from left to right, we would slide the starboard *guaras* deeper into the water, while pulling the portside *guaras* out of the water—or vice versa. The most important were the *guaras* at the corners of the stern. These would have to be shifted to compensate for winds blowing from an angle. Although basically simple, mastery of the technique is crucial to the successful steering of such a raft. Heyerdahl had known about the function of *guaras* but, perhaps because he could not read the Cervantesesque Spanish in which the Huancavilca accounts were written, he had not been able to make proper use of them.

The final addition to the raft contributed a bizarre touch. It was a tall dignified throne, consisting of several carefully carved panels of choice balsa wood, with a large hole in the seat like an old-fashioned privy. And that's exactly what it was—an amphibious toilet, which we perched on a special portside shelf that would hang over the water, assuring us of instant wash-away disposal.

Our raft completed, we proudly inspected our work. Not a single nail had been used, nor wire cable, nor metal spike. We wanted *La Balsa* to duplicate, as closely as possible, those ancient crafts that navigated the Pacific thousands of years before us.

3

The day we left port, about fifty or sixty friends and skeptics came aboard our little raft at Guayaquil to wish us well—or to shake their heads with undisguised dismay. One optimist was Señora Paladines, the wife of a local doctor. Wearing a floppy butterfly hat and a flowery blue dress, she carried in her white gloved hands a scrawny black and white kitten.

"I've brought you a present, Vital!" she exclaimed in a high breathless voice, handing me the tiny squirming animal. "It's a mascot, for good luck."

"But it's only a baby," I protested. "This is going to be a rough journey."

"Kittens are always good luck," she said, ignoring my comment.

"He'll need it," declared a local journalist standing beside her.

His cynicism apparently was shared by most of the people around us. One of the more vocal doubters, a potbellied old sailor, rubbed the multicolored anchor and hula dancer tattooed on his right forearm as he spoke. "This damned thing won't get nowhere. Two or three days is all I give her before these logs start soaking water like a damn sponge." The guttural harshness of his voice annoyed me, and I was glad to hear the doctor's wife cut him short.

"Nonsense," she said, "*La Balsa* will go all the way to Australia."

Grateful as I was for her kind intercession, I was not happy with the mascot she'd given us. We already had four pets: a much older cat, a large parrot, and two smaller parrots. I would have to get rid of this fragile little creature before setting sail. But I would have to be sneaky about it. After nightfall, before the tugboat picked us up, I would take the kitten on shore and give it away.

More pressing matters, however, demanded our immediate attention. Our secondhand radio suddenly went dead, both transmitter and receiver. We had planned to buy a modern apparatus from a local dealer, but we had run out of cash—and credit. Thus, we had to settle for an old radio that was a patchwork of several different brands—Japanese tubes, German condensers, American tuning device, and Ecuadorian adhesive tape.

"Perhaps it doesn't like Spaniards," said Gabriel when he saw me trying to make it work. "I'll fix it."

But his Chilean guile was ineffective, and we finally had to send an emergency call for Joe Megan, an American who happens to be president of one of Ecuador's largest electronics companies. It was he who had helped us locate and renovate our radio, warning us that it probably wouldn't transmit anything beyond a few hundred miles. "This bag of coils won't help you a bit on the high seas," he said. "You'll end up being deaf and dumb."

Megan was even more dubious about our wooden raft. Nevertheless, he good-naturedly responded to our plea and finally managed to get the radio to function as well as could be expected.

"It's still lousy," he said. "But I don't think you'll need it for very long, anyway."

We hardly listened to such talk as we loaded our storage area with fruits, hard biscuits, fresh water, kerosene, extra rope, a few books, survival medicines, and fishing gear. Gabriel, our student from Chile, dragged his tattered sleeping bag into our closet-sized cabin and stashed it against the wall. Then, every once in a while, before returning to shore for another armload, he would tighten the rope knots that fastened the bamboo cabin to the main deck.

Marc's special concern was the food supply. It was his duty, which he seemed to enjoy a bit too much, to curb the natural appetites of all the rest of us. Nothing that anyone wanted to take on board (pizza for Gabriel, mangoes for me) could meet his rigid specifications. "It's perishable," he would say. "It will spoil, there's no refrigeration." That he was right didn't make his "no" any more acceptable.

Nevertheless, in all the hectic activity of that final afternoon, I managed to eat three farewell mangoes, my share of the dozen we'd been given by Hernan Fernandez, an Ecuadorian cameraman who had come to film our departure. I savored every one as we carefully stitched Salvador Dali's beautiful painting over the sun I had painted on our sail. Dali had given us an emblematic portrait of our raft as a good-luck token, and we had decided to display it every Sunday if the weather permitted. But as a precaution against the sun and salt winds, we had encased his work in a clear plastic sheath.

Immersed in all these preparations, I completely forgot about the kitten Señora Paladines had given us. Not until several hours after we had gotten under way, when I felt its tiny paws crawling across my bare leg as I lay inside the cabin, did I suddenly realize our unwanted mascot was still with us. I let out a howl of anger.

"What's this damned thing doing here!" I yelled, lunging for it.

"Señora Paladines," whispered Gabriel, holding the kitten out of my reach. "She brought it—as a mascot."

"Well, she can't stay," I said, with a bit more composure. "I intended to give her away. To one of those kids at the wharf. But then I forgot all about her."

"Then he can stay?" asked Gabriel, having already ascertained the kitten's true gender. "He's a fine mascot."

"It's too damned little," I said. *"Mira,* Gabriel, it's only three weeks old! How can it possibly survive?"

"I'll take care of him," said Gabriel, turning to Marc and Normand for support.

"I'm sorry," I said, resenting the villain's role they were forcing on me. "We'll give it to the captain of the towboat."

"But you can't!" protested Gabriel. "He won't take care of it. Let me have him, Vital. I'll take full responsibility. I'll let him sleep with me."

Realizing it would be impossible to change his mind, I finally gave in. Let them learn for themselves, I thought. The cat smells would soon drive them crazy.

Much to my annoyance, this little creature, whom they christened Minet, was the only one on board that showed no

44

signs of seasickness during those first few days. Skittering around the deck on his tiny white paws, he looked almost perversely healthy, playing with the numerous crabs swept aboard by the waves.

"I hate healthy cats," I groaned, watching Minet scoot around the deck at breakneck speed.

"It's only a kitten," Gabriel reminded me.

"They're worse," I said. "They have no respect for sick people. He's flaunting his health just to annoy us."

Still, I couldn't resist the kitten's outrageous charm, or his refusal to be disliked which is typical of so many rascals. Consequently, when a huge wave gushed over the bow and caught Minet in its backwash, I jumped to the rescue, lurching across the deck and colliding with Gabriel and Marc, who had responded even quicker. When the wave receded, there was Minet clinging to the edge of the raft with his small, sharp claws buried in the outer log, shaking his water-soaked head and mewing like fury.

Lunging ahead of us, Gabriel grabbed the kitten as another wave loomed above us. Then, holding Minet in the curve of his stomach, he caught the spray on his shoulders. Crawling and stumbling back to the cabin with the kitten in his hand, he grabbed a towel and dried him off. "Don't cry, Minet," he mumbled in a half whisper.

Less than three hours after his narrow escape, however, Minet was back to his usual form, frisking around the deck in search of new adventure, teasing the crabs, pawing my trouser leg, hovering around Normand as he pulled in a large fiercely flapping tuna. After a while he noticed the older cat, Cocos, nibbling at some shredded fish Marc had given him. Abandoning the crabs, Minet scampered across the deck and muscled his way to the pile of fish, pushing the larger cat aside. Then, as Normand began slicing the freshly caught tuna with a butcher knife, Minet moved in and started lapping the blood off the deck as if it were milk.

Having been unable to consume anything but hot bouillon since we set sail, I was momentarily sickened by the kitten's appetite. Yet I couldn't help envying its lust for life. Unfortunately neither Minet nor Cocos were housebroken. They laid claim to one corner of the cabin and the resulting smell (mingled with the odors of four men living in tight quarters) soon became intolerable. "Gabriel," I said, "you promised to train those cats. Now look what we have—a real mess."

He smiled and shrugged. "I'll train them," he said. "I'll try harder now that I'm not so seasick."

"You'll never housebreak them," I said. "We'll simply have to keep them outside. That goes for the birds, too."

"Outside!" he protested. "But they'll get washed away."

There was a long painful silence, but I was determined not to give in, knowing that my low tolerance for odors would eventually result in deeper anger and resentment.

"I guess you're right," he said in a barely audible voice. "It's silly to fight about cats." Then, as if to convince himself, he grabbed Minet and Cocos from their customary corner and took them outside.

Fortunately, there were other matters to claim our attention. On the third or fourth day, Gabriel spotted a thick shoal of sardines hovering to starboard and yelled to us as he leaned near the water for a closer look. As we joined him we saw thousands of silvery creatures thrashing alongside us, sometimes nibbling at the balsa logs as if to ascertain what kind of strange sea animal it was. They were so absorbed in this occupation that they failed to notice a ten-foot shark slicing through the waves like a torpedo.

"Watch out!" shouted Gabriel, instinctively pulling back.

Even had the sardines understood him, it would have been too late. In one huge bite the shark consumed thirty or forty fish, then zoomed past us and whirled around swiftly for another mouthful.

"*Cobarde!*" shouted Gabriel, shaking his fist. "Damned coward!"

The shark made a third sweep past the raft, rolling over to show its white belly, rubbing against the starboard log, then dipping under us at a cross-angle as if to scratch its back on the barnacles which had already accumulated on the bottom.

"That's a mean bastard," said Marc, reaching for a harpoon. "Let's get him." But the shark disappeared as quickly as it came.

That same afternoon we were escorted by several large dolphins, scores of tunnies and bonitos, plus other species we couldn't identify. And toward sunset—an incredible burst of flame across the entire horizon—some flying fish came whizzing past our sail and plopped on deck, flapping toward the cabin as Cocos scrambled for cover. Minet, on the other hand, started circling one of the fish and pawing at it.

"*Cuidado,* Minet!" said Gabriel, holding him back by the tail. "He'll swat you."

But the hand-sized flying fish soon tired, their eyes stared helplessly at us as though resigned to whatever fate we decreed for them. The smaller ones we used as bait for the more edible thirty-pound dolphins, the larger ones were fried on a skillet. Useful as they were, they often proved a nuisance and sometimes a danger. During the day we could see them glittering in midair like silver projectiles arching toward us. At night, however, they would come winging through the air unseen, often crashing into our faces. One of them gave me a black eye that bothered me for a week, and the fact that Marc later turned the offender into a most delectable dish did little to salve my wound.

Other fish, mostly small species such as sardines, were tossed on deck by the waves, and one of the night watch's final chores at dawn was to collect them and set them aside for the day's meal. Occasionally Minet would participate in the roundup, and sometimes he would carry a sardine into the cabin as an offering to one of the sleeping crew. I thought it was immensely funny when he deposited two little fish in Normand's beard, but I was much less amused when he tried to feed me one in the middle of a prolonged snore.

By now we had become accustomed to the motion of the raft. Our seasickness had subsided, and we had all developed hearty appetites, especially when Marc prepared filets of shark stuffed with crabmeat. Most of the time, however, our seafood meals were plainer fare. Marc was the best cook; I was mediocre; Normand and Gabriel left much to be desired. Consequently, since cooking chores were evenly divided, we ate well every fourth day.

Shortly after dawn of our sixth day at sea, the wind shifted suddenly and blew directly from astern. Caught unawares, we struggled furiously to pull in the sail and were very nearly swept overboard before we managed to haul it down. The waves grew steeper and higher, pushing us forward at a breakneck pace, and our principal worry was the danger of broaching, twisting around broadside so that a breaker could roll us over. Finally, Marc decided to secure the main *guara* at the stern. By dashing among the others, first lifting one at the side then lowering another at the bow, we were able to keep *La Balsa* moving with the waves, which soon resembled rows of foam-capped mountains marching behind, then under and past us. Time and again the peaks would curl forward and splash down thunderingly into the trough we had just vacated. And once in a while, a huge "rogue wave" would break the rhythm, dropping tons of water against us broadside with a thundering noise that defies description. Had any of them hit us a few seconds sooner, the avalanche would have smashed our cabin like a straw hat. Fearing that possibility, we stayed outside, exposed to the elements, while the raft pitched, yawed, reeled, and spun around like a matchstick in a whirlpool. Finally we were forced to leave the *guaras* in what we hoped was the proper position, and we hung onto the crossbeams as the waves washed over us relentlessly, blinding us and incapacitating us completely. Fortunately, our steering worked by itself. The raft seemed to be under the control of some unknown force, cutting around the edges of the huge swells, racing ahead of the breaking crests, and swooping up and down as though we were on an air-cushioned toboggan.

Gradually the gale winds shifted away from us, the watery Alps diminished to foothills and finally became a rippling prairie.

"This quiet sea could become monotonous," said Gabriel after a few hours of smooth sailing.

"You don't have to worry," said Marc, his eyes closed against the glare of the noonday sun. "There will be more bad seas than good ones."

4

We were rapidly approaching the Humboldt Current, that broad cold mass of water that sweeps up from the Antarctic, runs north along the coast of Chile and Peru, and veers to the northwest just below the equator. As we reached its eastern fringe, toward the end of our first week, I checked the sea temperature. It is always lower than in more quiescent waters, but I found it much colder than I had expected for late spring and it was also a deeper, richer green, indicating an abundance of plankton, on which fish and other marine bodies live. Plankton feeds on nutritious plants in the water and dies off and sinks slowly to the sea bed when the water is cleared of these nutrients. The best sources of replenishment can be found near river mouths or shallow coastal waters; but in very deep seas there must be an upwelling of chemical-laden bottom water, such as is produced by a swift-moving current. Thus, since we would be riding with the plankton-rich Humboldt well past the Galapagos Islands, we would be assured of a steady supply of fresh fish.

Halfway to the Galapagos we began shedding our clothes, not by choice but by force of circumstance. With the waves and ocean spray constantly washing over us, soaking everything, we soon realized we wouldn't be completely dry again until journey's end. There were also frequent rains—often three or four days of cloudbursts in succession—which penetrated everything. We spent hours and hours wringing out our clothes and blankets until our hands ached, then slapping them against the twin masts or hanging them on the boom where they would dry—until the next barrage of waves soaked everything again.

Marc and I had already experienced the curious night-and-day extremes of the volatile equatorial climate, but Gabriel was convinced we were having a siege of unusual weather caused by atomic explosions in the Pacific. "I simply can't believe that you can freeze and catch pneumonia right on the equator," he said one night, pulling a blanket around his trembling legs.

"Don't worry, Gabriel," Marc said comfortingly. "After sunrise you'll long for the cold again."

Soon after dawn, we abandoned our shoes and sandals during the day; then our sweaters and shirts. Finally we started wearing skimpy loincloths, alternating them with shorts whenever we got them dry enough for comfort. Only on cold nights did we wear our damp clothes as partial protection against the wind.

The sun was always relentless and blisteringly hot. Rising to 115 degrees, the equatorial heat would make the cabin feel like the inside of a boiling teakettle. "I could poach a fish in there," observed Marc one afternoon as clouds of steam drifted through the doorway. "But I'm afraid it would be overdone." Thus, unable to shelter ourselves against the noonday sun, we would lie or sit helplessly on the deck, getting darker than the natives who had helped us cut down the balsa trees. We also got blisters from the unbearable heat, and our hair became so brittle and dry it felt like needle-sharp wire filled with electricity. Worse yet, Normand and I broke out with saltwater boils, small eruptions on our skin that itched worse than poison ivy.

When the sun disappeared and the night winds blew, the temperature would drop fifty or sixty degrees in a few hours. Once again we'd be shivering in the sudden chill, and all we could do was wrap ourselves in steam-dampened sweaters and blankets and huddle inside the cabin.

During our first few days in the Humboldt Current, we noticed that there were offshore winds in the daylight hours, but in the evenings the winds would shift to blow us back toward shore. These contrary winds were used quite effectively by the ancient Indian fishermen, whose big sailing rafts were taken westward thirty or forty miles by the offshore winds and then carried back at nightfall by an easterly breeze, but they gave us fits.

Now, favored by a steady southeastern wind, we sailed a course that would take us south of the Galapagos Islands at a slow, even pace that we periodically gauged by tossing scraps of paper or slivers of banana leaves into the water and then counting the seconds it took for the raft to move past them. If it took us 10 seconds to pass the marker, our 42-foot raft would be moving 84 yards per minute, thus covering a mile in 21 minutes, for an approximate speed of 3 miles per hour or 72 miles a day. For a pessimist, that yard-by-yard progress would have been disheartening—especially when one multiplies 8,500 miles by the 1,760 yards that make up a mile for a grand total of 14,960,000 yards—but none of us dared to think in such depressing terms.

As we moved into the swiftest part of the Humboldt the waves got bigger, making our footing somewhat precarious. One morning just after sunrise, as Normand was standing watch, he failed to notice a large wave breaking toward the stern. Coming at a slight angle, it caught the raft and rammed Normand into a pile of boxes, then washed him overboard before he could yell for help. Fortunately, he was able to scramble back on board after a frantic few seconds.

"What were you doing, chasing sharks?" I asked while he was drying off.

"Oh boooy," he said in an expiring whisper.

"Well, you can't chase sharks without a rope around your belly," I said, thereby establishing a rule that all watchmen must bind their waists with a long rope attached to the mast. Even as I spoke I noticed two sharks cruising about twenty feet behind the stern. They could have chewed Normand to mincemeat.

About an hour later I checked our course on the sextant. On clear days I would generally take at least three sightings of the sun: at sunrise, noon, and just before sunset. But that second hand sextant caused me considerable worry. Because of constant soakings in salt water, its mirrors were spotted and rusted around the edges, and one of them had been jarred loose when I dropped the instrument. Consequently, that particular mirror sometimes gave a false reading. If it was only slightly skewed the error would be minor and difficult to detect. But when there was a gross error, indicating an extreme maladjustment of the loose mirror, I might spend the whole day correcting it. Taking a sight every half hour, I would plot the resulting position lines on a chart and the numerous lines ultimately resembled a multiple-spoked wheel without a rim. A small, well-defined hub at the center indicated that the sextant was performing accurately; but a large open hub formed by crossed-over position lines was evidence of continued malfunction, requiring another day-long adjustment.

But even a perfectly accurate sextant is useless without a good chronometer. Prior to the advent of Harrison's Chronometer in 1735, mariners had to calculate their easting and westing by guesswork. One could judge latitude, since it could be estimated by measuring the maximum altitude of the sun at noon. But the calculation of longitude depended on knowing the exact time, to the second, when the sun's altitude was being measured. Before the chronometer, most ships sailed north or south until they reached the latitude of their destination, then turned at a right angle and pursued a direct course along that chosen latitude. But when Harrison invented a navigational timepiece that varied only three seconds a day in different climates, he made it possible for seamen to make accurate and simultaneous calculations of both their latitude and longitude.

Neither a sextant nor chronometer can help you, however, when the sun fails to appear. And perhaps it was only my imagination, but I distinctly felt that the sea was far more turbulent on sunless days.

When it was too rough, our helmsman would have to keep a sharp eye out for large waves. If an erratic crest threatened to break and crash over the deck, he would have to abandon the steering *guara*, run forward, and grab hold of the mast or a crossbeam to keep from being washed overboard. Then he would have to rush back to the *guaras* and set the raft on its proper course again.

Since there were four of us, each had two three-hour turns at the helm every twenty-four hours. The first few days, when we were still relatively soft landlubbers, were especially hard. Fatigued and muscle-sore, I would crawl into my sleeping bag after a particularly rough watch, and try to catch a nap. But inevitably, just as I managed to fall into a deep slumber, someone would pull the cord attached to my ankle to awaken me for some emergency. Thus, I was finding it impossible to shake off the high fevers that persisted long after my seasickness had subsided.

"You'd better lay off for a couple of days," Marc finally warned me. "You can't get well without sleep."

But I refused to follow his advice. Having seldom been ill, I foolishly believed that the best way to fight sickness was to ignore it. So I took several aspirins and continued with my share of work, drenched in cold sweat and suffering an occasional dizzy spell.

As things developed, I had no time to rest. A huge storm assaulted us close to sundown on the ninth day. It came in the wake of stiff southeastern winds, which shifted direction as they intensified, gradually forcing us north. Hoping to avoid the treacherous currents south of the Galapagos, we pulled in the sail and lashed down our *guaras* and hoped they would hold us to a westerly path. The waves grew bigger, forming white-capped walls ten or fifteen feet high.

Having seen how well the cabin sustained the onslaught of the first storm, we decided to take refuge in the relative protection it offered.

"Tie your waist!" I yelled, grabbing a rope to secure my own and tying the loose end to a post. "It's going to be rough!"

"What about Minet?" asked Gabriel, already holding him in his arms. "And the other animals?"

"I'll take Cocos," Marc volunteered. "Vital can take Lori, and Normand the smaller parrots."

Then it came. A huge mass of water loomed over us for several agonizing seconds, then crashed into the cabin at full force, hurling the raft sideways and spinning it around in a backlash. Cawing madly, the parrot I was holding tried to flutter out of my grasp; and Minet let out a frightened but angry meoww that pierced the thunder of onrushing waves. Then another meoww as the next wave gushed through the doorway and rocked us back and forth. Caught in the narrow confines of the crazily tilting cabin, not knowing when or where succeeding waves would come from, I felt like a blind man on a roller coaster.

Spurred by even stronger winds that increased after sunset, the waves kept battering us from all sides. But the bamboo walls of the cabin, bending to accommodate the onslaught of water, held firm throughout the two-hour storm, the knots of the ropes pulling tighter with the additional strain. When the sea finally subsided, however, the interior was chaos, our bedding strewn about like limp dishrags.

Gabriel (with Minet now perched cockily on his right shoulder) was the first to leave the cabin, beaming a flashlight in all directions for a quick survey of damage caused by the storm. The rest of us followed.

"Not too bad," said Gabriel. "We came off pretty well."

"Could be worse," Marc agreed, pursing his lips.

"We'll get a better look in the morning," I said, feeling

slightly dizzy again. "I'm a little worried about our course. Damned storm probably carried us too far north."

"Where's your compass?" asked Marc.

"Couldn't find it a minute ago," I said. "It's somewhere in the cabin probably. Under all that mess. I'll look for it tomorrow."

I dragged myself back to the cabin, hot flushes of renewed fever rising through my chest and head. Easing myself onto my wet sleeping bag, my shirt and trousers bunched into a soggy pillow, I felt even worse. "Think good thoughts," I kept telling myself. But the feverish images in my mind refused to yield to happy ones. I knew we were approaching the Galapagos, where my first raft expedition had come to a sorry end, and I kept thinking about that voyage. One of the men had been terribly frightened and wanted to leave us just three days out of port. Refusing to eat, he remained inside the cabin day and night. The fear of sharks and possible hurricanes had made him hysterical, forcing him to stay awake forty-eight hours at a stretch and reducing his usefulness to zero. Finally we sighted a large steamship that agreed to take him aboard, and we accepted his hurried resignation with relief. Shortly thereafter we came ashore on the Island of San Cristobal, where we met some nuns who urged us to continue our journey, and several days later we set sail again, hoping to move westward along the northern extremes of the Galapagos. But the winds and ocean currents decreed otherwise. Almost instantly our raft, the *Pacifica*, began to drift due north, then northeast toward Central America. Round and round we went, imprisoned in a huge loop of contrary currents and erratic winds, unable to get back to the westward swing of the Humboldt Current. Days, weeks, finally months went by, with no escape. No ships came near us. No islands appeared to offer us refuge. Our only contact with land was our often malfunctioning radio. Finally, the raft had begun to absorb water, the balsas rotting from the fermented sap that had gradually spread from the core to the outer surface of each log.

Lying there in the dead of night, wrapped in my wet sleeping bag, I recalled the final stages of that first trip. How well I remembered the sinking of the *Pacifica* after 143 days at sea, the frantic messages to and from the radio hams who had followed our progress, the maddening disintegration of each log as the choppy seas increased the friction between them, and the bizarre upward tilt of the raft as the stern gradually began to settle. We scrambled onto the roof of the cabin as several sharks slithered across the sinking logs, praying for help as the raft dropped lower and lower. Then, as the cabin itself began to founder, we were miraculously rescued by a German ship—just two hours before the *Pacifica* submerged completely.

I had relived that nightmare adventure many times. So had Marc, but both of us had been determined to try again.

The next morning, when I got outside, the sea was still running high, but the waves came in long even stretches, less chaotic than the night before. With the sun beating down on the matted deck and bamboo cabin, everything looked clean and bright. Gradually the sea grew calmer and the sun hotter. Piercing the eyes of two coconuts with a screwdriver, we drank a toast to the welcome change, savoring the cool milk like fine wine.

Marc watched me with paternal interest as I took a second sip. "You're looking much better, Vital," he said.

"I think so," I said. "I'm ready to read my maps again."

With Normand's help, I laid out the navigation map Admiral Fernandez had given me, and located our whereabouts with the aid of a compass and my second hand sextant.

My simple calculations indicated that the southeast trade winds and the Humboldt Current had been sending us on a course leading to the countercurrents around the Galapagos, that we had been heading due northwest at about fifty to sixty sea miles per day. Once again we were faced with the possibility of drifting into the treacherous eddies south of the Galapagos, where we could be shifted off course by strong currents swirling toward Central America, taking us back to the trap where the *Pacifica* finally sank. In a few moments, I ascertained the direction of a new breeze blowing from the southeast. Then, with great caution, I swung the sail a few degrees to the west, holding the full wind inside the billowing canvas but nonetheless shifting our path from northwest to northwest-by-west. With luck, we would swing west across the sea with the main current, ten or twenty miles south of the Galapagos.

"I wish we were going closer," said Gabriel. "I've been told that the islands are beautiful."

"They are," I said. "But bad luck for Marc and me."

I described in detail the dramatic impact one gets seeing the jagged black lava rocks rising out of the sea, polished for centuries by Pacific waters and gleaming in the equatorial sun like black diamonds. I also told him about the multicolored lizards, skittering in and out of the porous stone and changing color like capricious runaway gems. There were flightless cormorants waddling along the coast, hundreds of albatross laying eggs and hatching their young, strange little red-footed birds called "boobies," marine iguanas that looked like miniature prehistoric monsters, and playful sea lions body surfing and drying themselves to a light beige on the hot sand.

"There are also enormous turtles in this region," I said.

"I know," said Gabriel. "Normand caught one this morning."

He pointed over his right shoulder. "It's back there. We've got him tied to the stern, upside down. But we've got to let him go pretty soon—some damned seabirds keep pecking at his legs and neck. And Minet keeps jumping on his belly."

"Nonsense!" I protested. "We'll have some turtle soup."

"I've got a better idea," said Marc. "We'll use him to attract other fish. The dorados are always chasing turtles. We'll drag it along behind us in the water."

After debating how best to harness the creature, which was at least three feet in diameter and much too heavy to bear a rope around its neck or legs, Gabriel hit upon the idea of drilling a hole through his shell and tying a rope through it. Lacking a real drill, he heated up a screwdriver till it was red hot and burned a hole through the back end of the shell. Securing a strong line through the hole, we lowered the huge turtle into the water behind the stern, and within ten minutes a procession of dorados, tunnies and sardines were trailing after us. That evening we had generous servings of *Dorado L'Modena,* since it was, fortunately, Marc's day to cook.

After supper we all sat on the matted deck in front of the cabin, playing Parcheesi and speculating about the weather. During a lapse in conversation, I became acutely aware of a continuous creaking and groaning under us, a prolonged barely audible screech now and then, and grating noises all around us. I knew the sounds were caused by the perpetual movement of logs shifting with the waves and the constant pull and strain on the hundreds of ropes holding the raft together, but I hadn't fully realized how much friction was involved in the never-ending strain between rope and log—the deck, the crossbeams, the mast, the cabin, the *guaras,* hundreds of movable parts constantly straining. No raft built with nails and screws, with immovable parts, could have lasted very long on these waters. Yet I was compelled to ask myself how long the ropes could withstand the ceaseless pressure. Would they gradually wear away, strand by strand? Or suddenly break?

The next morning I examined a few ropes on the crossbeams and was relieved to find they were in excellent shape, firmly snuggled in their respective grooves on either end of the main logs. I was also happy to note that the balsa wood showed no signs of excessive wear. Later checking the hemstitched borders of the sail, I detected no shredding from the intense winds we'd gone through—but the sun I had painted in the center was somewhat faded from the sun and salt breezes.

Aware of my scrutiny, Marc touched the lower margins of the painting. "I think it'll last a while," he said. "At least till Samoa. But I'm glad we've got the Salvador Dali painting enclosed in plastic. The salt winds would ruin it."

"How did you get him to paint it?" asked Gabriel.

"Ask Vital. He's the one who promoted it."

I had been convinced from the outset that we needed a fine painting for our sail, something that would inspire us all the way to Australia. Being a Spaniard, I naturally wanted to have it painted by one of my countrymen—either Picasso or Dali—and I wanted it as a gift offering to our success. We could not have afforded even a pencil sketch from either of these artistic giants. I soon found out that Picasso would be impossible to reach, but I learned that Dali might be accessible, that he had a suite at the St. Regis Hotel in New York City, where he sometimes sat in the lobby apparently engaged in that ancient sport of "people watching." So I got in touch with a friend who worked for the Spanish U.N. mission, and he managed to get me invited to a large social function where Dali was to be present. Taking a plane from Montreal, I arrived in New York several hours before the reception.

But something strange and unsettling happened when I was introduced to Dali. He declined to shake hands. When I extended my right hand, he merely bowed slightly from the waist, folding his own two hands behind his back as if he disdained human contact. Later on, I was told that he will shake hands with no one on first meeting, but at the time I was too self-involved to notice how he had behaved with others. Consequently, I took it as a personal affront and completely lost my composure, failing to mention the painting I wanted from him.

Several days later, sitting at a bar in Montreal, I suddenly decided to call him long distance. But I was informed by the St. Regis switchboard operator that Dali had gone to Spain. Undaunted, I somehow managed to get his phone number in Madrid and immediately called him. Not until later did I realize that it was three in the morning when his phone rang.

"Aalooo," said a sleepy raspy voice.

"Is this Salvador Dali?" I asked.

"I think so," he said, sleepily uncertain.

"This is Vital Alsar," I said. "The man who is sailing a

raft from Ecuador to Australia, and I want to talk to you about a painting for my sail. I forgot to mention it in New York."

A long silence on his end of the line.

"Maestro? Are you still there?"

"Yes, I'm here."

So I proceeded with a breathless spiel about my need for a talisman for my projected journey, stressing that I couldn't pay for it. When I had finished there was another long silence.

"Did you hear me?"

"I heard," said the raspy voice.

"Will you give me the painting?"

An agonizing silence pregnant with refusal.

"*Olé*," he said, his voice coming to life. "*Olé! Olé! Como tienes cojones, hombre. Si te lo doy.*"

It's impossible to convey the sound of his voice, but he told me I had a hell of a nerve—and that he would give me a painting.

Several months later, in the presence of numerous reporters and TV newscasters with klieg lights and cameras, Dali spread out a canvas on the floor of a hotel banquet room and painted an "instant masterpiece" for *La Balsa*. It was a rather abstract painting of a raft, a heart, and a huge sun against a background that resembled two massive *cojones*, the eternal Spanish symbol for courage and daring.

"I've got a Jewish friend who would call that a prime example of *chutzpa*," said Gabriel when I had finished my story.

"Whatever it is," I answered, "we've got the painting."

Later that afternoon, when I crawled into the cabin, I saw Minet sitting there facing Dali's painting, which we had

63

strapped against the rear wall. Hearing me come in, he whirled around halfway, then stopped, like a burglar caught redhanded, the loose end of a green string, which we had used to hemstitch the painting, in his paw. Suddenly he bolted for the doorway, dragging the string behind him until it drew taut and tripped him. Quickly slipping the string off his claws, he scrambled through my legs and made his escape.

"There goes a cool kitten," I thought. "And a born delinquent." It was hard to believe that he was less than five weeks old.

During dinner I was about to tell Gabriel and Marc about Minet's latest stunt, but I was interrupted by a familiar raspy sound. It was Gabriel and his spoon. With every bite he would crunch his teeth into the base of the spoon—crack!—then scrape the food off with his upper front teeth, producing a "rasssp" like a shovel on bare cement. Craack—rassp—craack—rassp . . . all through every meal. It was beginning to annoy me almost beyond endurance. But, according to the rule I myself had decreed, I couldn't complain to him about it. Worse yet was the way Marc ate on the days when Gabriel or Normand cooked. He felt, with good reason, that Gabriel used too much oil in his cooking, and too many spices. Normand overcooked or undercooked everything. Adhering to our no-personal-criticism rule, Marc would show his disdain for their food by dropping his lower jaw after every chew, letting it sag for three or four seconds, and then swallowing with a painful effort. Normand, with his natural inclination for solitude, would always eat outside the cabin, even when it rained. So I felt like a lone martyr at meal times during the entire trip.

Occasionally, when my nerves reached the breaking

Workmen strip bark from balsa tree as Don Cesar, right, supervises.

Logs are maneuvered to get the closest fit possible.

The balsa logs—with shallow grooves neatly carved for the hemp ropes that will bind them together—are lined up on the pier in Guayaquil. No nails, nuts, bolts, or other metal parts were used in construction of the raft.

Normand wields a skillful hatchet and chisel.

Heavy beams are tied across the logs to hold them together.

l and Normand secure
rigging. Sail was
ted by Vital.

Vital with mascots. Four
of crew's five pets died
enroute.

alvador Dali's painting, which was hoisted only on clear days.

Normand, Gabriel, and Vital haul in a vicious-looking shark.

Minet stares hungrily at a dorado.

Balsa (opposite) under sail.

Gabriel relaxes in doorway of the raft's small bamboo cabin.

Marc and Normand debate best way to prepare a flying fish.

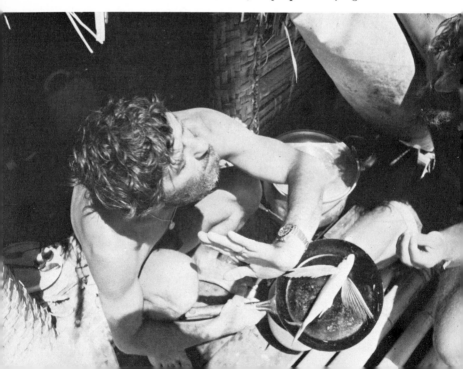

point, I would sneak off to my favorite retreat behind the cabin. There I would sit on the storage box and brood for an hour or two about all kinds of personal annoyances and grievances against my crewmates, staring at the slowly receding waters of the vast Pacific as my pent-up emotions gradually subsided.

We all had favorite retreats on the raft, where we would go to nurse a private grief or anger, and no one was bothered at such times. Normand's was the starboard corner of the bow; Marc's was on the portside edge of the stern; and Gabriel would always sit inside the cabin. The length of time we spent in our individual "hideaways" would vary from a half hour to several, and the only one who dared to intrude was Minet. But after a while, even he seemed to realize that a man's retreat was more sacred than his castle. In fact, he himself had a retreat, the forward tip of the cabin roof, where he would sit on his haunches, immobile as a gargoyle.

5

By the grace of God and strong southeastern winds, we managed to skirt the southern fringe of the Galapagos without being snared in the treacherous crosscurrents as we had feared. But our luck soon came to an end.

Our pets began to die. One by one, they succumbed to a strange viral infection that I later learned was something akin to psittacosis, or parrot fever, a deadly and highly contagious disease carried by certain birds and readily transmitted to other animals—as well as to humans.

The parrot Fernando was the first to go, gradually giving in to the sickness that attacked him not long after we left Guayaquil. He had enjoyed an occasional respite from what Gabriel called "the little bugs," but most of the time he lolled about the raft in a semi-stupor or simply slumped in a limp sleeplessness on the floor of his cage. He had shrieked a few swear words on our first day at sea, but after a while he could barely manage a weak phlegmy *aaark*. Finally, on June 16, he fell dead in a small pen we'd built for him near the bow, where he could be isolated and still have more space to move around. With the familiar personal vulnerability one always feels in the presence of death, we put Fernando back in his cage and slowly lowered him into the sea. Then we watched it rocking back and forth under water, gently sinking to the bottom as a hundred sardines converged upon it, slithering through the cage and nipping the parrot's feathers.

Cocos, the older cat, was the next to die. He had been sick, off and on, from the very beginning. Marc had given him all the fish scraps he could eat, but he consumed very little. Apparently infected by Fernando's virus, he moped around most of the time, feebly resisting the devilish pranks of the younger kitten. How he must have resented Minet's good health and blithe spirit.

"You can't kill a kitten that drinks shark's blood," Marc had observed one morning when Minet was skittering around the sleepy prone body of the larger cat, vainly trying to start a game of tag or hide-and-seek. "There you have the perfect symbols of life and death."

A few hours later Cocos crawled into a corner of the cabin and quietly lay down to die. Minet was nuzzling his neck and face, apparently trying to awaken him, when I discovered the body. We wrapped him in a bag and lowered him into the water close to the bow, hoping to save him from the crowd of fish trailing the stern. But a minute later we noticed a furious thrashing about ten or twelve feet below, behind the stern, as the hungry fish attacked the corpse.

The parrot Isabel was the next victim. She died on a Thursday night, and we found her lying next to Lorita the following morning. They had been in the same cage since Fernando's death. Lorita had frequently pecked her, but Isabel had continued to snuggle up to the larger parrot for warmth at night.

"She's gone to join Fernando," said Gabriel as he put her into the water. *"Que Dios te bendiga."* (May God bless you.)

Then turning his attention to the remaining parrot, who was also very ill, Gabriel assumed the role of ship's doctor, although his practices were somewhat unorthodox. He tried to cure Lorita with wine and song, crooning an ancient Chilean lullaby as he poured wine down her forced-open beak. Two hours later she was madly jumping and flapping around her cage, and we were momentarily convinced that Gabriel's medicine had worked. But then she let out a loud raspy squawk and flopped to the floor, instantly dead.

It was such a weird turnabout, so totally unexpected, that we were all visibly shaken. Marc quietly wrapped her in an old blue shirt and tossed her overboard as far out as he could. But almost instantly we saw an eight-foot shark slice through the water to grab the unexpected feast.

It was a grim reminder of what might happen to all of us, and I was in no mood for such reminders. My own viral infection had refused to respond to large doses of aspirin, and I had acquired what I assumed to be a severe case of bronchitis. (Actually, as I learned at the end of our trip, I was probably suffering from the same disease that had killed all our pets except Minet, but fortunately I didn't know at the time the grave danger I was in.)

My resting pulse, normally 74, was down to 54. Weak

and limp, mentally depressed, I saw everything in shades of gray. When I tried to play Parcheesi, the dice felt like hunks of lead in my palm.

Trying to sleep in the middle of the night, I could hear the beating of my heart above the noise of shifting logs and creaking ropes—as if it were the only part of me that was still alive. I was to suffer this way for forty-five days, hardly able to leave the cabin for fifteen of those days, but determined to hang on. One afternoon, when an antibiotic I was taking had a particularly adverse effect, I really thought I might die, that I would never get to Australia. But eventually my fever subsided, the dizzy spells became less frequent, and though I remained weak for a while, I was able to leave the cabin more frequently and stay on my feet for longer periods of time.

I could see the relief in my crewmates' faces as they noted my improvement. They never said so, but I'm sure there were times when they thought my fate would be that of our four pets. Perhaps to celebrate my return to the living, Gabriel set up an experimental washing machine (he knew my mania for cleanliness), which was fully automatic and required no electricity. By hanging his pants and shirts between the logs so that the onrushing waves produced a natural agitation under the raft, he got a fairly effective "salt-water wash."

"I'm going to patent this and start a new business in Chile," he said. But on the fourth or fifth washing, his pants were torn to shreds, and he gave up the idea. "It's all capitalist nonsense anyway," he said.

Having broached the subject, he launched into a long lecture on the glories of socialism, declaring that Salvador Allende, the new Chilean President, would soon lead his country into a great era of social and economic reform. Inevitably, he started to criticize the United States government, which provoked counterarguments from Marc and me.

"The United States isn't so bad," I said. "They have some fine people there—and more freedom than almost anywhere in the world."

"How can you say that, Vital," he protested, smacking the steering oar for emphasis. "Look how the black man is treated, for example. And what about the poor?"

"Poor people are treated pretty badly everywhere— even in Latin America."

We would go on like that for hours, our voices rising, our fists pounding. One such argument was cut short one night by the sudden appearance of a huge pair of gaping jaws with a double row of sharp-fanged teeth, moving toward our starboard side as if to bite off a chunk of raft six feet wide. I have no doubt that the gleaming teeth could have chewed through the balsa logs like a giant rip saw, but the jaws slowly closed and seemed to back away. Rushing toward the edge of the raft, we saw an enormous "sea monster" with a broad flat head like a toad, two ridiculously small eyes on the sides, and huge jaws, now clamped shut and forming large jowls. His entire body was covered with phosphorescent plankton, so that he was clearly visible in the moonlit night. On the crest of his immense body was a dorsal fin that projected high above the surface, perhaps five or six feet, slashing up foam whenever he pivoted.

"*Mira,* Minet," Gabriel whispered to the fascinated kitten on his shoulder. "There you have the ugliest thing in the world."

"And look at all the fish hanging on it," said Marc as its giant body, perhaps twenty-five or thirty feet long, swirled

70

around us, with hundreds of small phosphorescent remora fish clinging to it. There was also a mass of pilot fish swimming in front of it, reminding me of armed henchmen preceding a powerful underworld figure.

"Are they running interference for that ugly monster?" asked Gabriel. "Or is he simply following them because he's too dumb to know where to go by himself?"

The answer came almost immediately. Diving suddenly, the creature lost his lead escort, but the little striped fish quickly dived after him and had regained their up-front position when he reappeared near the bow. They're like a blunch of yes-men, I thought, frantically trying to second guess the bossman. Ironically, this role decreed their ultimate demise. All the creature had to do to get rid of them was to zoom forward a few feet and gobble them up in a single bite. As for the parasite fish and crabs stuck to his body, however, he was probably as helpless as a bull elephant with fleas on his hide.

From our later descriptions of him, I was told he was probably a whale shark, a pelagic species that is said to reach a length of seventy feet, often weighing as much as twenty tons. The one we had seen was only half that large, but we all felt it could be terribly dangerous if aroused.

"One hefty swat with that tail could tear this raft apart," said Marc. "So don't anger him."

Nodding his head gravely, Normand leaned over for a closer look as the giant shark hesitated beneath us, nuzzling the barnacles on the underside of the starboard logs and tilting us slightly to port.

"The sonofabitch is teasing us," I said.

Then, as the huge body rolled and heaved under the bow, the entire raft rocked back and forth with a loud creaking and rasping as the logs strained against the ropes. It was a tense moment, and I later wondered if that squint-eyed monster could actually have a sense of drama, a dim primordial love of suspense. For at least twenty suspenseful minutes he remained directly under *La Balsa,* rocking it from bow to stern, all of us standing close to the cabin doorway waiting for the sudden heave that would surely capsize us.

Finally, tired of the suspense, Marc reached for a thirty-pound dorado he'd begun to slice for dinner and flung it as far as he could off to starboard. Immediately the striped "escort" fish trailed after it, and the monster followed them.

"You're a genius!" I said to Marc.

"I'm a damned fool," he growled. "I should have done that ten minutes ago. But I didn't want to lose that dorado. Best damn fish I've seen in a long time. Now we won't have *Dorado L'Modena* for supper. Just plain ordinary tunnies."

His tuna dishes were never ordinary, nor was anything else he cooked. But on that particular occasion I had a yen for something really different, a meal that required no cooking. Recalling a Japanese dish I had once eaten called *sashimi,* I asked Marc to cut several thin slices of raw tuna for me. Then, in imitation of the delicate soft-spoken waitress who had served it to me, I arranged the slices in a flower formation on my plate. Only one thing was lacking—the sauce. But I had brought a bottle of Ecuadorian hot sauce called *aji,* and, carefully setting my plate inside the cabin, I went back to the storage box near the stern to look for it. Two minutes later, returning with the sauce in my hand, I found Minet chewing the last piece of my tuna.

Grabbing him around the belly, I yanked him away and put him in the bird cage vacated by Lorita's death. I tied a long rope to the hook on top, climbed the masthead, and looped the loose end of the rope through a pulley. Then I slowly lifted Minet to the top of the mast.

"What the hell are you doing, Vital?" yelled Gabriel. "That's crazy!"

"I'm punishing him," I said. "You guys have spoiled him rotten."

The mast, which rocked back and forth even on quiet seas, was tilting more than usual, so that the cage was swinging way over the water, first to starboard and then to port. Minet let out a furious meow, which brought a chorus of protest from Marc, Gabriel, and Normand.

"Stop, Vital! Get him down," said Marc. "He's liable to fall out."

Evidently sensing that his allies outnumbered me, Minet raised the volume of his meows as the cage swung over us— back and forth, back and forth. After about the twentieth swing I lowered the cage, and Minet glared at me through the bars with a mixture of fear and resentment.

"He's going to hate you," said Gabriel, opening the cage and taking Minet into his arms.

"He'll also respect me," I said.

There was no further talk for a considerable period. I guess we knew that any further discussion about Minet would lead to anger and recrimination.

The following evening, after toiling over our little stove for more than two hours, Gabriel served us filets of tuna floating in a goo of highly spiced grease, accompanied by a huge mound of black beans. Tackling the beans first, I swallowed two mouthfuls before I realized they had a most peculiar taste. Smelling them, I detected the unmistakable odor of kerosene.

73

"Gabriel, you've poisoned us!" I yelled, feeling an instant nausea.

"What's wrong?" he said, calmly chewing a mouthful.

"The beans! They have kerosene in them."

Pausing to get a careful taste, he finally said, "You may be right, Vital. They do taste a little different, I better check."

He left the cabin and I followed.

Though it is difficult to believe, he had actually cooked the beans in kerosene instead of water, mistaking the gasoline can for the water jug. How he managed not to cause an explosion or fire is something only his angels can explain.

Strangely enough, Normand had detected nothing unusual about the beans and would probably have eaten them all if we hadn't told him. Even then, his only reaction was a slight shrug.

Although I had become accustomed to his silence, his manner that evening disturbed me. When Gabriel and I laughed about his mistake, Normand simply stared beyond us at the darkening waters, his eyes totally blank. Even Minet failed to evoke a response when he rubbed up against Normand's legs.

"Something's wrong with our friend," said Gabriel when we were back in the cabin.

"I'm afraid so," I said. "He's been that way all day."

"Maybe he's thinking about his girl friend back in Montreal. Or some family problem," said Gabriel.

Whatever it was, it continued to plague him for the next few days. Not even the strong winds that tossed us about for five hours west of the Galapagos could force him out of his solemn mood, though the rest of us were cursing and laughing as we struggled to keep *La Balsa* from drifting due north. His response to any order ("pull in the sail—hold the *guaras*—fasten the steering oar") was purely mechanical, like a bearded robot.

"We've got problems," said Marc after the storm, when Normand was out of earshot. "He's liable to become seriously withdrawn, like that man on our first trip."

He was referring to the Ecuadorian who had left our raft, *Pacifica,* just before we reached the Galapagos. The man had fallen into a deep melancholia, staring out at the sea for hours at a time, eating less and less. He had finally secluded himself in the cabin, refusing to come out, refusing to eat, refusing to say a single word to any of us. He would spend all day with the same book, reading the same page for a whole week.

Now we were faced with the onset of the same syndrome, in our own "Homme du Bois." Marc had told me that Normand was perhaps the quietest man he had ever met. "I have known him for many years," he confided. "Yet he's told me very little about himself." From other mutual friends, he had learned that Normand was a native of Montreal, but no one seemed to know who his parents were or if he had any brothers or sisters. He had apparently studied to be an architect but was somehow sidetracked and became a draftsman instead. We also knew, from bits of conversation here and there, that he had spent many summers sailing boats on little-known rivers in northern Canada, often camping alone for weeks at a time.

Though we had become accustomed to his passion for silence, the withdrawal he now suffered was most disturbing. Somehow, we had to break into that inward-spiraling cycle before it was too late. It would be disastrous to have him breakdown on the raft. I had visions of him finally succumbing to a serious state of immobility, unable to care for himself in a storm or a raftwreck. Or perhaps he would go to the other extreme, suddenly bursting into a raving anger and violence that none of us could deal with. Either possibility was fraught with danger. In any case, we knew we had to act, however naïvely or unprofessionally, to forestall the breakdown that seemed to be threatening.

On the third day of his strange faraway mood, I saw him standing near the stern with his eyes fixed on the far horizon.

"The Eiffel Tower is to your left, monsieur," I said in my best Parisian French. "Or perhaps it's of no interest to you people from Marseille."

There was a flicker on his lips, a faint hint of a smile, but not a word.

An hour later—once again relying on my amateur theories of psychological problems—I walked up to him with a prim ramrod severity.

"I must collect your passenger ticket," I said. "We can't allow any stowaways on this ship."

No response this time, not even a twitch; but I persisted.

"I don't *care* if you own the ship, monsieur," I said. "Either give me your ticket or you'll be booted off when we get to Melbourne."

Again, the same expressionless indifference. Still mindful of his ever-so-slight reaction to the Eiffel Tower gambit, I walked around the cabin and approached him again.

"*Voilà!* Another Frenchman on board!" I exclaimed. "You must be from Marseille. I know your father—General De Gaulle, the most intelligent midget I've ever known."

There was a faint smile on his lips, but nothing in his eyes.

Clearly, we must try something more dramatic, something that would force his involvement. Perhaps a bit of psychodrama would help. I called Gabriel and Marc into the cabin, and we quickly worked out a free-form script that we put into production that same afternoon. Our stage was the cooking area directly in front of the cabin.

Taking a flying fish from the kitchen basket, I cut off its head and started to slice it with a butcher knife, knowing that Minet would soon come around to lick up the blood. Sure enough, within a few seconds he was squirming between my legs to get at the red puddles around my shoes.

Cursing him in French and Spanish, my voice raised to frenzied pitch, I grabbed Minet and threw him across the deck, straight toward Normand. By reflex action, he reached out and caught him. Still feigning rage, I rushed toward them, yelling, "Give me that goddamned cat—I'm going to drown him!"

"Like hell you will," snarled Normand, holding me back with one arm. "He's my cat."

It worked; we had broken through. Suddenly Normand grinned. "Oooooh boy," was all he said, but it was music to our ears.

He might have pulled out of his melancholia without our intervention, but I'm inclined to think we helped him somewhat. Though it was happily resolved (Normand never once lapsed into another siege), the incident reminded us again of our limitations. What, for example, would we do in case of serious illness, a traumatic injury such as a shark bite, or perhaps sunstroke?

Anticipating these contingencies, I had gotten some practical training from a group of Mexican doctors who were personal friends and patrons of our voyage. Among them were Dr. Carlos Fink, Dr. Ezequiel Alvarez Tostado, Dr. Carlos Gomez Medina, and Dr. Petry Choly. It was Dr. Fink and his lovely wife Norma, an American from Oregon, who arranged for me to see several surgical operations at local hospitals.

"I want you to get used to blood gushing from open wounds," Carlos told me. "The open tissues and bones of the human body look a lot different in an operating room than in the color photos of a medical textbook."

They certainly did. I particularly remember the bruised and shredded thigh muscles of a man who had been struck by a bus turning a corner. I had stood near the surgeon, watching his deft, skilled hands as he removed the dirt and grime, realigned the muscle tissues, and sutured them. That same afternoon, wearing a fresh white smock and surgical mask, I looked in on an amputation. The patient was an elderly man who had had an arterial obstruction in one arm, and because of the lack of circulation it had become gangrened. Feeling a bit squeamish, I watched as Dr. Fink painted two curved lines on the arm and cut along them, leaving two long skin flaps. He cut the muscles and pulled them away from the bone, which he carefully sawed through. After tying the small bleeding vessels, he covered the bone and sutured the muscles over it with catgut, then sewed the skin with black silk. He performed the delicate operation with complete mastery, his sensitive fingers handling the tissues and nerves with artistry and precision.

That kind of firsthand exposure to surgery had made me keenly aware of both the strength and the vulnerability of the human body. It also impressed upon me the frightening possibility that I myself might be called upon to perform a primitive approximation of some of the surgical operations I had seen. Bearing that in mind, I kept our butcher knife sharpened to a keen edge at all times. What worried me most about the prospect of performing major surgery on the high seas was the continuous motion of the raft, even on the calmest seas. Not for one second, from Ecuador to Australia, would we be totally still. Surély, there is no medical school that takes that into account.

I naturally tended to worry most about shark bites, not because they were really most probable but because we were constantly aware of the sharks' presence. Toss an empty can from the raft and a shark was there to snatch it. A piece of wood or paper—another shark. They were always there, waiting and watching.

In the Humboldt Current they had been blue in color; now that we were past the Galapagos they were brownish gray. The longest were about fifteen feet, but the most dangerous were only seven feet long. Menacing at all times, they were generally more active either very early or late in the day, when their bellies were empty. During the voyage we harpooned about one hundred sharks, killing thirty and wounding seventy or more. We had to kill them to keep them from scaring away the fish that followed us. Those fish were our natural refrigerator, which we had to protect in order to survive.

Since the sharks' food was on the surface, they generally swam with their fins jutting out of the water, enabling us to spot them at a considerable distance. But sometimes we couldn't see them until they were practically on us, bursting out of the sea like rockets. One afternoon about mid-June,

Gabriel was cleaning a tunnie near the stern, squatting on the hindmost crossbeam with his back to the water, when suddenly a huge wave carrying a six-foot shark washed over the raft. The shark's nose bumped against Gabriel's hip, knocking him six feet against the rear wall of the cabin. Assuming someone was playing a joke on him, he shouted in mock anger, "What kind of game is this?"

Then he noticed the shark, floundering on the deck. *"Mira, el monstruo!"* he said. Eventually, Marc brought it under submission with four or five thrusts of a double harpoon.

It was always dangerous to kill one on board because you could never be sure it was really dead. You might bend over an apparently inert fish, only to be suddenly clobbered by a swat of its tail. Once we cut one open and took out its pulsating heart, holding it in our cupped hands and feeling it throb for several minutes. Sometimes a shark's heart will stay alive that way for more than a half hour.

Their will to live was incredible. I remember a seven-foot shark that trailed us for several miles, west of the Galapagos. We had laid out a line for dolphin with a tuna head on the hook, and he was apparently waiting for the larger fish to appear, stalking us with all the persistence of a well-paid private detective. Finally, when a fairly large dolphin swallowed our bait, the shark zipped in and chewed off its tail. Marc reared back and rammed his double harpoon into the shark's back, but although blood spurted from the wound, the shark kept snapping at the dolphin. Once again Marc harpooned him, and still the shark hung on. Again and again, Marc drove the harpoon deep into its body, but the monster never stopped until he had completely devoured the dolphin. Then after a last desperate lunge that spurted blood in all directions, he stopped struggling and died.

"I'll bet his heart's still pumping," said Gabriel. As we were speculating on that possibility, a couple of smaller sharks, attracted by the smell of blood, arrived on the scene.

"Here goes!" Gabriel shouted. "They'll chew him to bits—and probably kill each other fighting for the biggest share."

Marc shook his head. "No, they won't touch him. Sharks never eat each other. No matter how hungry they are."

As if to verify it, the sharks merely sniffed the mangled corpse of their less fortunate brother and disappeared. A few minutes later a swarm of smaller fish surged through the still-bloody waters to devour the abandoned remains.

That night, as I lay half asleep with an acute resurgence of the high fever that still plagued me from time to time, I was suddenly aware of a strange noise. Hundreds of teeth seemed to be gnawing on the logs outside the cabin. Slowly crawling out of my sleeping bag, I crept through the doorway and saw thousands of fish nibbling at the edges of our raft, just like the swarm of parasitic fish that had devoured the dead shark. They were clearly visible in the bright moonlight, with their eyes, unblinking and neon green, staring at me from all angles, thousands of eyes bobbing up and down with the waves. Then—as someone behind me shouted my name—they all disappeared.

It was Marc. "Vital! What are you doing out here?"

"There were thousands of fish," I said, shaking my head. "Making a strange noise."

"There's nothing there," he said. "Just a lot of plankton. You must have had a nightmare. You've got a fever again."

It was, indeed, nothing more than a fever-induced hallucination. I've been told that sailors, especially those who travel alone, often have vivid and recurrent hallucinations. The American sea captain Joshua Slocum, on his solo voyage aboard the *Spray,* had numerous visits by a ghostly figure who claimed to be a pilot for Christopher Columbus on the *Pinta.*

I'd like to think that it was the ghost of Juan de la Casa who visited Slocum. He was a sailor from my hometown of Santander, Spain, the man who drew the maps for Columbus' first voyage to the new world. In my childhood I was forever reminded that America might never have been discovered without the help of Juan de la Casa, "the pride of Santander." He was always on my mind whenever I sat on my favorite lookout point on the rocky coast just north of that city of some 150,000 souls.

I went there often as a child, sometimes to take out a rowboat on the choppy waves or to go fishing for *jargos* and *lubinas,* two regional fish similar to sea bass and bluefish, and for eels. At the age of twelve I sneaked out of school one afternoon and went on a three-day outing up the coast, fishing at night and sleeping most of the day on a huge flat rock above the bay. It was a marvelously solitary experience; long quiet days of complete communion with the sea. Ordinarily, my father would have punished me for not coming home at sundown (he always insisted on a seven o'clock curfew for me and my older brothers Lazaro, Nemesio, and Pedro); but on this particular occasion, he merely shook his head and sent me to bed. Perhaps he was simply relieved that I hadn't drowned or been kidnapped—or run away on a merchant ship.

There was, of course, no reason for me to run away

from home. I had a perfectly happy childhood, fishing, rowing, hiking along the coast or in the mountains with my brothers, attending soccer matches and bullfights with my father, and teaching my little sister Marina how to shoot marbles with her left hand or how to make a kite with ordinary newspaper.

Often in those early years I used to watch the men go off with the fishing trawlers into the Bay of Biscay, the treacherous *Cantabrico*, where the sea is very high and fierce. And I remember the women wailing for the men who did not come back, as the reports came in—ten men lost at sea, sometimes twenty or more. The harshness of the sea was etched into the character of these people—pessimistic, brooding, rugged—and I loved the fishermen; they were brave, goodhearted men. Yet they feared the sea, they allowed it to dominate them.

Later, in 1954 or 1955, I read a book by Dr. Alain Bombard, describing his solitary, sixty-five-day crossing of the Atlantic in a collapsible life raft. It showed how man can survive if he knows more about the sea. In the most vicious cyclones, it is not the wind and sea alone that kills men, but fear, terror. Often a man's heart will stop before he touches the water. But if a man takes the sea as a friend, not an enemy, if he learns from childhood to respect it, it will respond in kind.

During one prolonged period of my childhood everything was interrupted by the Spanish Civil War. Night after night the city of Santander, controlled by the Republican Loyalist forces, was bombed by German airplanes flying close to the rooftops to avoid high-flying shrapnel. Whenever we heard the warning sirens everybody would rush out of their homes and run to a factory near the *Barrio del Rey*, the neighborhood we lived in. The factory was the only building near us that had a bomb shelter. But one night our whole family was delayed in reaching the shelter, my little brother having been unable to find his shoes, and just as we were rounding a corner a block away from the factory, it suddenly exploded and burst into flames. A Nazi plane had made a direct hit, killing everybody inside the two-story building. Later on my father learned that half the bomb shelter was used as a munitions dump.

Though we were lucky to escape death, we were to suffer considerable hardship during and after the war. In 1941, for example, a cyclone ripped through Santander, destroying miles of overhead electrical cables, which caused hundreds of fires that ultimately destroyed two-thirds of the city. Homeless, ill-fed, and lacking medical care, at least one-third of my friends and close relatives subsequently died of tuberculosis. Those years were among the most terrifying for all Spaniards, and I shall never forget the suffering I witnessed all around me.

Yet in spite of certain family hardships, I managed to graduate from Colegio La Salle, a Catholic school, at the age of sixteen, and thereafter spent a miserable three years at La Academia Puente, a commercial school in Santander where I finally got into a fist fight with a headmaster who habitually beat students for talking too loudly or failing to wear a proper tie.

Then in 1954, anxious to see the world, I left home and signed up for a twelve-month hitch in the Spanish Foreign Legion, where I became a full lieutenant at the age of twenty-two. Hoping to gain some experience and perhaps see a bit of action, I asked to be sent to North Africa. Assigned to a post in Ceuta, Morocco, my battalion had to guard some munition dumps along the Moroccan-Algerian border, alternately fighting off attacks from Algerian rebels and local thugs trying to rob guns and ammunition for contraband sales to those same rebels. While there, I came across a Spanish edition of *Kon-Tiki,* which I managed to read during a few quiet moments between snipers, and I was so impressed with Heyerdahl's account of his voyage halfway across the Pacific on a raft that I began mulling over the possibility of sailing my own someday. I was particularly fascinated with his idea of duplicating the ancient balsa rafts used by the Hauncavilca Indians.

Before I could realistically consider such a project, however, I had to complete my education and find something at which to earn a living. With the idea of becoming a language professor or perhaps joining the diplomatic service, I decided to take up the study of modern languages and enrolled at the Alianza Francesa in Paris. To pay my tuition, room, and board, I worked as a longshoreman, waiter, and furniture mover, attending classes after work and studying far into the night. But the ocean adventure was never far from my mind. About my second year at the Alianza, I read the French translation of Heyerdahl's book and was more determined than ever to sail the Pacific on my own. My friends thought I was crazy then—and probably still do.

After three and a half years of fairly intensive lessons in French, I went to Stuttgart to learn German. Six months later I moved to Hamburg, where my brother Pedro was studying economics at the university, and earned my keep as a riveter and welder, working high up on the steel scaffolds of large office buildings. During my three years there I managed to burn and permanently scar my hands and feet with red-hot rivets, and once nearly fell from a twenty-story scaffold when my heel slipped on an ice-caked crossbeam.

"Father was wrong about the sharks killing you someday," Pedro said one night. "You won't live long enough."

"Nothing will kill me until I've crossed the Pacific," I said.

By now the idea had become an obsession, and I had decided not to delay any longer. Perhaps I would become a language professor later, but for the moment I had a dream to pursue—to build my own balsa raft and sail it across the Pacific. Of course such an expedition would cost money (even with all my bumming and scrounging of free supplies and materials it would run about eight thousand dollars), and when someone at the construction company where I worked told me there were good, high-paying jobs in Labrador, I needed no persuasion. "You can save almost every cent you earn," he had told me, "because room and board are free." Obtaining a visa from the Canadian consulate in Hamburg, I boarded a plane for that formidable region of northern Canada. It was fifty degrees below zero when we landed, and the plane almost skidded off the icy runway. But it was even twenty degrees colder at the iron mines at Wabusch Lake, where I worked four months and lived in what seemed like a huge concentration camp—four thousand men and not a single woman. We all dressed like bears for work, in thick fur coats and hats, huge fur-lined boots, and two pairs of extra-heavy corduroy pants, all furnished by the company. It made everyone look like Frankenstein's monster, lumbering along stiff-legged from side to side and blowing clouds of steam into the bitterly cold air.

Most of my fellow workers were tough, rugged men,

with enormous appetites and no particular fetish for table manners. In the overheated company cafeteria, where the temperature often rose to ninety or a hundred degrees, I once watched in fascinated disbelief as a huge bearded lout helped himself to four big steaks, a half pound of potatoes, several servings of peas and carrots, gobs of thick gravy, and seven or eight slices of bread, all of which he devoured in less than twenty minutes. And I must admit that I also ate more—and with more gusto—than I've ever eaten in my life. Yet somehow I managed to retain my usual weight, probably because I was also working harder than ever—ten hours a day, seven days a week. Unfortunately, I did not get along well with my foreman, a vocal advocate of Naziism, and one afternoon, after a heated political argument, I was unceremoniously dismissed.

Though I had managed to save almost all of the four thousand dollars I had earned, I was still considerably short of my goal, so I went to Montreal and got a job teaching Spanish at a local Berlitz school. I was later offered a professorship in the foreign language department of the University of Montreal, but by that time I had almost enough money, I had met Marc Modena, and we had agreed to undertake a voyage across the Pacific.

We did not, of course, make it on that first ill-fated expedition of the *Pacifica* in 1966. But far from dampening my enthusiasm, that experience redoubled my determination to make a successful crossing, and four years later, after again scraping together the necessary funds, I was ready for a second try aboard *La Balsa*.

6

Early in June, as we were breezing along on a westerly current far beyond the Galapagos, we had several nights of intense fog that worried us. My charts indicated that we were crossing through certain shipping lanes, and we all realized the danger of a nighttime collision with a vessel that might not see our feeble lamps until it was too late to avoid us. Fog, particularly at night, was to be one of our worst and most constant enemies. I particularly remember an incident that occurred later in our voyage, when we were just west of Huon Island.

We were sailing through a thick patchy fog—the visibility ranging from five feet one minute to two hundred feet ten minutes later—when Marc noticed some lights directly ahead of us. As they got larger and brighter, he realized it was a large ship moving toward us at considerable speed. We had only a small night light to indicate our presence, and suddenly even that was extinguished by a strong wind. Grabbing a flashlight, Marc tried to signal the approaching vessel, but the beams were apparently thwarted by the fog and the high-rolling waves, for the ship kept coming straight at us. Now, desperately fearing a collision, Marc jumped onto the cabin roof with a Bengal flare, but the wind kept blowing out his matches.

"Let me try," I yelled, reaching for the flare. "There's less wind down here."

I managed to light it, but completely botched the job. Instead of going up, the flare went down, ricocheted off the deck, narrowly missing Minet and the gasoline can he was perched on, and sizzled into the sea.

Meanwhile, Marc had finally managed to light two simpler flares and shot them upwards, but by then the ship loomed ahead of us like a rhinoceros bent for destruction.

"Get ready to jump!" I yelled, knowing it was probably too late.

But it wasn't necessary. The ship angled to the right, charging past us at full speed, creating a chaos of waves that hit us broadside.

"That was a real miracle, old man," I said to Marc, grabbing the mast as the raft took the impact.

When the waves had subsided, we could see, through a break in the patchy fog, that the ship had stopped about two miles away. "We'd better let them know who we are," I said. "They saw our flares, but I'm not sure they saw the raft."

The ship slowly came back toward *La Balsa,* its crew exchanging more signals with us. When it got close enough, Marc and I hopped into our rubber dinghy and started rowing toward the now motionless vessel, beaming our flashlight so they could tell we were coming. I was hoping to ascertain our latitude (the day before, skies had been too cloudy to get a reading) and perhaps get a bit of kerosene to replace the two quarts Gabriel had wasted on the beans. But as we drew near the ship, it began to move away.

"They don't see us," said Marc. "We'll have to catch them."

Doubling our efforts, we rowed for about a half hour, swearing with every stroke. Just as we were about to cave in with exhaustion, someone spotted the dinghy through the murky darkness and the ship came to a stop. To this day, I can remember how difficult it was to climb the rope ladder that was lowered for us, the racking pains in my arms and back, the burning in my chafed and swollen hands.

Once on board, we were taken directly to the captain's cabin. He was a slender, militanty erect Chinese with the coldest eyes I've ever seen. "What do you want?" he snapped, in a clipped, faintly accented English.

"I want to thank you for not killing us," I said. "And to apologize for causing you to stop. I know how expensive it is."

"It certainly is," he said, in the same hostile tone.

"But now that we're here," I continued, checking an impulse to punch him, "could you tell us the latitude?"

Consulting his chart, he read us the latitude, then added, without looking up, "All right, that's all."

"Could you spare a little water?" asked Marc. "And perhaps a little rice?"·

I was sure Marc expected nothing from this arrogant man, that he was merely testing a personal hunch—which proved to be correct.

Staring at us with cool disdain, the captain, whose name, we learned, was Fung, turned to one of his officers and snapped, "All right—give them a kilo of sugar and two kilos of rice. No more!"

Some of the crew later told us the captain had not wanted to stop for us once he saw we were only a raft, but his European engineer had reminded him that according to maritime tradition he *must* stop for anyone in distress. Unlike Fung, the crew was fascinated by us, asking all kinds of questions about the raft and our future plans. They also offered us cigarettes and fresh water.

About a half hour later, when we were getting ready to leave, I approached the captain again and said, "Our raft is about three miles from here, and with all this darkness—I wonder if you could take us part of the way?"

He nodded, unsmiling, and gave an order to his first mate. But when the ship started toward the raft, which was a barely visible point of light on the dark horizon, one of the sailors noticed that our dinghy was missing.

"The rope must have slipped loose," he said.

Rushing to the portside rail I stared into the night in search of our dinghy, but could see nothing.

"Do you really need that rubber boat?" asked the captain as if it were a useless trifle.

"It's the only one we have," I answered.

"We'll use our lights," said the first mate.

The ship circled round and round, its two huge spotlights probing the dark water, and the dinghy was finally located about two hundred yards away. By then Captain Fung was furious, and I couldn't blame him. Still, I thought he might let us use one of the lifeboats to go after the dinghy. But in spite of pleas from his crew, he was intransigent.

"If you want your damned dinghy," he said, "you can swim for it!"

Knowing the ship's lights might have attracted sharks, I thought he must be joking. But one look at his eyes told me he was dead serious.

"All right," I said. "I'll swim for it, and you'll have a good show, captain."

"You can't!" protested one of his mates. "It's too dangerous, man."

"There may be sharks," said another.

I climbed down the rope ladder seething with anger and sick with fright. Halfway down I dived as far out as I could, desperately flailing my arms the instant I touched the water. Expecting a shark at any moment, I swam those two hundred yards as if the devil himself were chasing me. A few feet away from the dinghy I thought I saw a dorsal fin slicing toward me, which goaded me into a final furious effort. Seconds later, I reached the dinghy and flopped inside.

Then, with less than two minutes' rest, I started rowing back to the ship, which seemed to be drifting away. Numb with pain and fatigue, I rowed like a robot, and finally managed to reach the ship. But when I started up the ladder, my aching muscles couldn't sustain me, and on the ninth or tenth rung I lost my grip and fell back into the dinghy.

As I was about to grab the ladder for a second try, I saw Marc starting down. Captain Fung had ordered him into the dinghy with the few supplies the crew had given us. He was abandoning us at least two miles away from *La Balsa*.

"That dirty swine," said Marc, shaking his fist toward the upper deck. "Who needs his lousy help!"

Had I been less angry and more honest, I would have said, "*We* do."

"I'll do the rowing," said Marc. "You'd better rest a while."

But water kept splashing into the dinghy, and I had to bail it out while Marc rowed. The waves were so high we kept losing sight of the raft's lantern, which flickered off and on as the winds got stronger. Worse yet—the fog was back again.

"We're going to lose them," said Marc. "We've got too much cargo on this thing."

So we dumped the rice, sugar, and three-gallon jug of water, leaving us only two bottles of rice wine, which one of the sailors had given us. Then I took up the oars and we both rowed, straining every muscle and gritting our teeth against the numbing pain. Finally, after more than an hour and a half, we reached *La Balsa,* and our crewmates hauled us aboard. We flopped on the deck in exhaustion. Later, Normand and Gabriel told us that Captain Fung's ship had passed very close to the raft, going full speed, and they wondered if something horrible had happened to us. It was a hard night's work for two bottles of rice wine.

It certainly brought home the danger of sailing our raft near regular shipping lanes. Had the fog been uniformly dense rather than patchy, the pilot of Fung's ship could not have seen our flares, and *La Balsa* would have been smashed to bits.

Although we could not foresee the incident with Captain Fung as we sailed on west of the Galapagos, the fog continued to worry us until about the middle of June, when it finally lifted. The next few days were comparatively calm and free of stress, giving us an opportunity to study the amazing variety of marine life around us. We were especially fascinated by the bright phosphorescence of the plankton, which turned the sea into a vast bed of glowing embers and streaks of fire at night.

"The first time I saw it," Gabriel confessed, "I was afraid it would burn me."

The "embers" were actually tiny shrimp and barnacles, and the "streaks of fire" were dolphins and tunnies diving and whirling under the raft. But the most spectacular mirages created by the phosphorescence were the strange lights we saw two or three hundred yards away, whirling coils of flame skimming the surface of the ocean.

"Those are dolphins chasing each other in circles," said Marc.

"You're crazy," said Gabriel. "They're flying saucers."

Although Marc's view was more probable, anything seemed possible in the eerie night life of the sea. Many times the dark waters around us would suddenly come alive like a discotheque with strobe lights shooting shafts of color in all directions, but we knew they were merely sardines scattering every which way to escape a hungry shark, his teeth illuminated in an angry, ragged arc.

The daylight hours were equally absorbing, though somewhat less dramatic. All kinds of fish, mollusks, and serpents constantly swam or floated around us, washing up on board with the high waves. Minet was especially fond of the small squid that would wiggle over the deck, flailing their ten arms in confusion whenever he pawed them. One afternoon a baby octopus was swept onto the deck, and Minet reached out his paw to trap one of the wiggly tentacles. But the octopus suddenly wrapped himself around the cat's leg and couldn't be shaken off. Surprised and frightened, Minet scooted around the deck, trying to knock it off, and I finally pulled it loose and tossed it back into the sea. In the commotion, we almost knocked over the pan of rice that Marc was preparing for dinner.

"Damn it," he growled, "you'll spoil my experiment!"

Always on the lookout for new ways to tease our appetites, he was making a casserole of rice and barnacles, with oregano, thyme, and several other spices.

"You're using *barnacles?*" I asked him, thinking of the thousands of sailors who have spent millions of hours scraping barnacles from ship bottoms all over the world. But of course only a French chef would know how to make good use of such seemingly useless nuisances. Needless to say, the casserole was delicious. Had he used a bit of saffron, it might have tasted like a poor man's paella.

It was such a tasty meal that Gabriel felt compelled to try another of *his* culinary experiments. "I have a new invention," he told us a few days later. "I'm going to cook beans in a pressure cooker. They're much better that way." First, he explained, he would heat the beans and water until they started to steam; then he would seal the pot so the steam wouldn't escape.

"How will you do that?" Marc asked.

He smiled as if he'd anticipated the question. "I'll strap the lid tight with my belt, then wrap the pot in my sleeping bag so it will stay hot. In an hour or two the steam will cook the beans. That way we'll keep all the vitamins and the flavor, too."

Of course, the steam easily escaped from the pot, and Gabriel sat there on his haunches, glumly watching the failure of his newest contraption, as it thoroughly soaked his sleeping bag.

When he opened the pot, the beans were still hard as pebbles.

"Maybe you'd better cook them the regular way," ventured Marc. "And don't forget the salt."

If Normand had been cooking, it wouldn't have been necessary to mention the salt, since he always overdid it, often using a couple of spoonfuls when a pinch would have been enough.

Bad as it was, however, we ate most of the food prepared by Normand and Gabriel. It had nutritive value if nothing else. Consequently, in spite of our high-protein seafood diet, none of us seemed to lose weight. We probably weren't exercising enough. At the beginning we did push-ups, knee bends, and other calisthenics, but we eased off after a while, convincing ourselves that our regular chores would keep us in shape. Our legs stayed firm and muscular because of the constant movement of the raft, which caused a continuous stress and strain on our calf and thigh muscles. Our stomach and shoulder muscles would have benefited from daily swimming in the ocean, but the continuing presence of sharks and swordfish ruled out that possibility. We had to restrict ourselves to brief two-or-three-minute plunges that afforded little exercise.

"I can't believe it," Gabriel said. "All this water—and we can't even swim in it."

Gabriel's desire to swim was satisfied sooner than he expected. That night he was sitting near the stern on his regular three-hour watch, passing the time with full-throated recitations of Pablo Neruda's poetry interspersed with Chilean folk songs, when he was cut short by an enormous jolt. A large wave heaved the raft to portside and hurtled him overboard. Totally surprised, he thrashed about for a few moments, then started swimming back toward *La Balsa,* only to be thwarted by a large and playful dolphin that had come from behind and started nibbling his toe. By now the raft had surged ahead fifteen or twenty feet, and he had to swim furiously to catch it.

"I thought it was a shark," he later told us, "and it boosted my adrenalin."

Awakened by the same jolt, we had rushed out of the cabin and were waiting to haul him out as he reached the rear crossbeam. He was covered with phosphorescent plankton from top to bottom, and glowed a bright amber.

"Someone get me a towel and a bandage," Gabriel growled. "That damned dolphin bit my toe."

It was only a minor wound—it had hardly drawn blood —but though he later laughed at the incident, he was somewhat shaken at the time. Relieved that he hadn't drowned or been eaten by sharks, I neglected to ask him why he hadn't tied a rope around his waist as we were all supposed to when we had the night watch. I thought of it the next morning but decided it would be better not to broach the subject until after breakfast, since his noisy eating habits annoyed me so intensely that I could never discuss anything dispassionately. But to my surprise, he didn't bite and scrape his spoon as usual. Nor did he at lunch or dinner.

"Have you noticed how quiet Gabriel has been eating today?" I asked Marc that evening.

"It's that swim he took last night," said Marc. "I think it relieved some of his tensions. He never made noises like that in Guayaquil; it all started when we took off. It isn't bad manners, it's just pent-up tensions."

Forever analyzing our various personal quirks, Marc often sounded like a professor of psychology. He was, in fact, a self-educated man with very little formal schooling. Born in the village of Frejus, France, near the Italian border, he had been captured by Nazi storm troopers at the age of fourteen and was immediately interned in a concentration camp. Finally escaping after three unsuccessful attempts, he joined the French underground Marquis forces when he was fifteen and served as a secret gun runner for two years. Then, at seventeen, he got a job on a merchant ship and visited nearly every major port in the world during the next four years, learning a thing or two about women of diverse cultures and reading a vast number of paperback books on an even greater variety of subjects. Still yearning for adventure, he joined the French Navy on his twenty-first birthday and was soon involved in the French-Indochina war, transporting troops and removing injured soldiers, ultimately reaching the gloomy conclusion that it would be an interminable war.

Having seen so many people at their best and worst and having lived through so many gut-tearing experiences, Marc had become a very wise man at an early age. Consequently his soft-spoken observations always commanded a certain attention and respect.

Realizing that I myself had been (and would be) under considerable strain, I wondered how he would analyze whatever quirks I had acquired. I have always been accused of hypercleanliness, which might be considered a Freudian symptom of submerged guilt. Perhaps my finicky aversion to bad smells was another aspect of the same phobia. In any case, my constant washing and cleaning up, especially around the cooking area, became intensely annoying, I was to learn later, to my three crewmates.

Unfortunately, the therapeutic value of Gabriel's spontaneous swim soon wore off, and within a few days he was back to his ear-grinding *craaack* and *raaasp*. Had we been able to get regular music on our radio I would have played it at top volume to drown out that noisy spoon; but we were limited to the episodic messages we got on the short-wave radio Joe Megan had fixed for us. Our only communication was with a few ham radio *aficionados* who kept in touch with us most of the way.

About two weeks after we left Ecuador we started hearing from Liliana, a woman from Guayaquil who operated a ham radio with the code letters HC2IS. She had a soothing voice, full of warmth and subtle enthusiasm.

"She talks like music," Marc said wistfully.

She tuned in our wave length every time we went on the air, promptly indicating her presence as if she were perpetually waiting for us.

"I forget everything for you men on *La Balsa*," she once told us, "my husband, my children; I live now only for the raft."

Calculating the time differentials as we got farther west, I realized that she often tuned in way after midnight. How could one resist such loyalty?

"When we get to Australia," I promised her one night, "we'll get you a big koala bear."

Listening to Liliana's soft beautiful voice telling us how much she worried about us and how often she prayed for each one (including the kitten), we inevitably started to speculate about her. How old was she? What did she look like? How did she dress? Marc was sure she was past thirty but under forty, stressing that no one could be that charming without having lived at least three decades.

"She's also slender, tall, and brunette," he added.

"Nonsense!" protested Gabriel. "She's a blonde with gray-green eyes and full heavy lips. She's shorter than me—about to here."

"She's fat, fifty, and funny," I said, to tease them. "She has black hair that's been dyed orange. She's also homely; only a homely woman can be that charming."

Actually, in my own mind Liliana was the very essence of beauty. Usually I envisioned her as gracefully slender, thirty-two years old, dark-haired, olive-skinned, witty and wise and enormously sensual. On other occasions she was blonde and buxom. Marc and Gabriel had their own ideas about her, endlessly speculating on the shape of her nose, the precise color of her eyes, and even the possible irregularity of her bite, oné of them reiterating a preference for slightly buck teeth.

"I don't really care what she looks like," Gabriel finally confessed. "I'm in love with her voice."

The other radio hams evoked less passionate responses. My good friend Vice Admiral Samuel Fernandez was always in close contact with *La Balsa* through XE1EB, a ham station in Mexico City. From Guadalajara, Mexico, we had continuous messages of concern and support from Rafael Corcuera, whose code number was XE1EEI. In San Diego, we had a faithful *aficionado* named Julio Ereneta. There were others who kept track of our progress by asking our position and charting it on naval maps. Admiral Fernandez was especially dedicated in this regard, time and again warning us against a southward drift that might carry us into a dangerous reef or a northward drift that could take us away from desired currents or wind patterns.

"*Pon atención,* Vital," he would say in his deep grandfatherly voice. "Don't go off on a fancy whim."

Occasionally, Admiral Fernandez and the other radio hams would arrange direct communication between one of us and a member of our family. Two or three times I was able to talk to my wife, Denise, who was always cheerful and full of good news about our two little daughters. She carefully avoided any mention of my mother-in-law's continuing skepticism and disapproval.

On July 10, a radio ham in Santiago de Chile managed to arrange a conversation between Gabriel and his mother. (Since Gabriel had not written to her before we left Guayaquil, I had asked my Guadalajara friend to contact the ham in Chile.)

"*Gabriel, mi hijo, cómo estás?* (How are you, my son?)," she said with a quaver in her voice. "I hope everything goes well with you even though you never write me."

"I'm fine, Mama," he answered. "We're nearly halfway and all goes well. But we can't talk long on this radio. *Adiós, Mama.* Say hello to all the family. Give them a hug for me. And please don't worry."

There was a brief pause, and then her anxious voice again: "Is there anything you need, my son? I'll send it right away."

Luckily, the circuit was cut just then and she could not hear our laughter at her wonderfully naïve offer.

"You should have asked her for a washing machine," said Marc. "Or at least some soap."

Had it been possible, I think Gabriel's mother would have sent him anything he asked for. She was a German baroness whose grandparents had emigrated to Chile during the French Revolution. His father, a poet and one of Chile's most distinguished musicologists, had died a few months before Gabriel joined us, and Gabriel, their only child, was now the main focus of his mother's life. "She has a few cats to keep her company when I'm traveling," he told me one evening. "But there's no one to read poetry to her now. She undoubtedly misses that."

Gabriel had enjoyed an easy, happy childhood in an upper-middle-class section of Santiago. He studied geology at the University of Chile and was active in student politics, attending numerous rallies in support of Salvador Allende and occasionally getting into minor scrapes with the police. Then upon graduation he and two friends started on a transcontinental hitch-hiking tour of South America, thumbing their way through Argentina, Uruguay, Paraguay, southern Brazil, Bolivia, Peru, and finally Ecuador, where we met him at a community action center established by the U.S. Peace Corps. "We were helping the Americans design a new irrigation system for some local farmers," he later told me. "And they gave us room and board for a couple of days." When we went there to ask for volunteers to help us build the raft, Gabriel was the first to offer his services.

A couple of days after Gabriel's talk with his mother, we hit a dead spot in the Pacific. There were no winds, not even a breeze; the sea was like a stagnant pond, with no currents moving in any direction. Our sail was hanging limp and the raft drifted at a snail's pace on no particular course, while the harsh equatorial sun beat down relentlessly.

"We're going nowhere," said Marc.

"The saints have abandoned us," I said.

For two days we sat; the temperature was one hundred and fourteen degrees in the sun. Drugged and drained by the fierce heat, unable to tolerate the fetid cat smells and body odors inside the cabin, we slouched around the deck like winos on a waterfront, scarcely talking to one another. Without the raft's motion to attract them, the dolphins, tunnies, sardines, and sharks had disappeared, compounding the weird desolation of the waters around us.

"This could drive you crazy," said Marc when the sun had gone down on the second day. "It's like living in a vacuum."

"I think I feel a breeze," I said, with more hope than conviction. "Should be better tomorrow."

Taking the first night watch a couple of hours later, I started worrying about Normand again. He hadn't said a word since the day before. Nor had he eaten very much. (In fact, none of us had.) I could see him standing still near the bow, staring into the darkness, his face a blank mask in the pale moonlight. The god-awful torpor and heat could easily trigger another siege of withdrawal. It was enough to drive anybody mad.

Fortunately, the next morning we had a change in the weather. A stiff westerly breeze puffed our sail like a pigeon's breast and thrust the raft forward at a good clip. Our revived spirits were reflected in the following entries in my log:

July 14:

We covered 132 miles yesterday, 5½ miles per hour for a 24-hour stretch. Once again we prove it's possible to navigate well in a raft. The current is very strong and the wind from the east. We are accustomed to being constantly wet. My sickness has almost gone. Marc has just checked the food supply and we have very little left—maybe not enough to reach Samoa. We shall have to live on nothing but fish or perhaps soups made from plankton. Fortunately, the fish are easy to catch. We can take them by hand.

Today a sperm whale surfaced ten feet away from the raft. He was 25 feet long, with huge jaws and long sharp teeth. But he meant no harm. He stayed with us all day.

Reviewing my log for that day, I also remember the playful squeaky dolphins that were around us almost constantly. In ancient times it was believed that dolphins were once human beings, a theory that's not too difficult to accept when you have seen them close up as often as we did. They seemed extremely social and gregarious, usually traveling in groups of seven or eight, swimming side by side in perfect harmony. Often called "the littlest whale," the dolphin is perhaps the most approachable of all sea animals, but for that very reason, he is also the most vulnerable.

Jacques Cousteau, the brilliant Frenchman who has made a lifelong study of marine life, says that dolphins are highly sensitive and never like to be alone—that they will brood and get sick if suddenly abandoned by their fellow dolphins. He also believes they communicate with each other in a language consisting of squeaks and whistles, which we ourselves often heard as they circled our raft, leaping over the waves in unison like chorus girls. They were so friendly and trusting that we were always reluctant to catch them, but the needs of our stomachs were stronger than our sympathies.

July 15:
Normand in good spirits.

Many sharks around us. I was lying near the front of the starboard log today when a shark zoomed past us, his head out of the water—*WHRRR!* He missed me by about twelve inches. I had seen him a few seconds before some twenty feet away, swimming high in a .wave about ten feet above the raft. I think he saw me down there and decided to come alongside *La Balsa* for a closer look.

July 17:

Good fishing. Hundreds of flying fish, with dolphins chasing them. Also lots of tunas and sharks. Everyone on board smells of fish, especially Minet.

July 19:

Winds steady, but currents erratic again.

On a raft you really get the feel of the sea—a feeling you can never have on a ship—because you are actually *on* the sea itself, in close physical contact with it. You can feel the currents, the changes in temperature. Sometimes you can actually see the fingers of a new current rippling toward you, often at speeds of 10 knots or more. And the new current could be colder or warmer than the one before it. The water temperature sometimes changes abruptly—particularly near the equator—from 25 to 35 degrees in just a few seconds.

The sea was always playing strange tricks on us. Near Samoa, for example, we would chart our position with the sextant early in the morning, and twelve hours later our sighting at sunset would show that we had traveled only thirty miles. Then in the next twelve hours—with exactly the same winds, no change in direction or velocity—we might cover forty-five to fifty miles. At first I couldn't figure this out. Why, under seemingly identical conditions, did our speed vary so greatly? Then we began to notice some peculiar habits of the fish: in the mornings, we could see the tuna swimming fifty meters below us, where they would remain all day, but at night they would rise so close to the surface we could feel them bump the raft. Of course, they were following the plankton-rich currents on which they fed. And so we had our answer to the mystery of our erratic progress: the currents in this area move like serpents, rising and falling, carrying us ahead swiftly as they rise, leaving us to drift more slowly as they fall.

July 20:
    The fish were particularly playful and plentiful this morning, but as usual, they disappeared at supper time.

That was another strange thing. On days when the fish were feeding near the surface, we could reach down and touch them. They would roll over and we'd scratch their slick bellies; they showed no fear whatever. But invariably, just before sundown, when whoever was chef that day was readying the frying pan, those same friendly fish would suddenly swim away. They seemed to sense the danger. I believe our intentions were actually transmitted to them through the nerve endings of our fingers. (To those who doubt this amazing sensitivity, I can only cite the recent scientific experiments with plants, which suggest that they, too, respond to friendly or unfriendly treatment.)

I'm convinced that you must become a part of nature to feel nature. You must become one with the sea, one with the fish. The sea is like a woman—soft, wild, sweet, moody. You can never understand these changes of mood. It is like your first love, pure and virgin, stormy and turbulent—always testing you and confounding you. If you want to conquer the sea, you must first prove that you are really strong. She will push you to the limits, but if you come through, she will open her arms and protect you.

My log entries continued to show the bounty of the sea.

July 21:
    Many sharks today. The dolphins have been on the rampage since early morning. Often we could tell when sharks

were near by the activity of the dolphins. They usually travel together, ten or twelve to a school, and when they are pursued by sharks, they jump high out of the water and come down with a resounding slap that frightens the predators away. They also feed together, jumping up after the flying fish like torpedos. Sometimes they work in concert, pushing 200 to 1,000 flying fish ahead of them, corraling them toward another school of dolphins waiting with open mouths. One has to admire such discipline.

July 22:

Minet jumped between my legs on the front log and went overboard this morning, into a very rough sea. Marc jumped in after him, and I grabbed Marc's ankles before he was completely in the water. He grabbed Minet, and I pulled them both in chain-fashion. We all looked like wet rats.

Though I failed to mention it in my log, I had terrible pains in my back that evening, a sudden culmination of needling aches that had plagued me for days. I was sore from the dampness and the constant lurching of the raft, and my hands were raw from handling the ropes in wet windy weather. Moreover, my nose was severely sunburned, the flaky skin peeling around the nostrils and exposing a second layer that was too tender for the blistering sun and salty breezes. None of these physical ailments, which we all suffered, were enough to keep me from my regular duties, but I nevertheless neglected to make any entries in my daily log for at least a week. Then, at last:

July 30:

Today we pass 142 05' W, the longitude of the *Kon-Tiki's* final landing on Raroia Reef after its 4,300-mile voyage from Peru. *La Balsa* has taken 62 days compared with *Kon-Tiki's* 101 days, and we are passing Raroia 1,000 miles to the north.

7

It would be false modesty to minimize the pride we felt in having duplicated Thor Heyerdahl's historic voyage on the *Kon-Tiki*. But now we faced the most difficult part of our journey, the treacherous expanse of the South Seas. Almost every sailor who has traveled the Pacific has his own story to tell of the dangerous 4,300-mile passage through the Samoa Islands, the Fijis, the New Hebrides, and the Saumarez Reefs. There are hundreds of reef barriers, most of them uncharted, lying in wait like submerged traps, and the hurricanes and cyclones in that area have made matchwood of many a ship.

Here, then, was the real test. We wanted to prove that the Incas and Huancavilcas could have navigated some of the most difficult waters of the seven seas in balsa rafts like this one.

"The *Kon-Tiki* started to fall apart about here," Gabriel reminded us. "How can we be sure about this raft? We've got the same kind of logs—"

"Not exactly," I interrupted. "Ours are lighter. Less sap in them."

I was sure it was the sap that had caused the *Kon-Tiki's* trouble. It had begun to ferment, rotting the logs from the core to the outside. But Gabriel was still skeptical, so we decided to have a look.

Three hours later, after carefully puncturing each log below water level, we were happily assured that they were in excellent shape, having absorbed almost no water.

Gabriel smiled broadly, boasting that we would easily outstrip Heyerdahl's larger raft and crew of six.

"We'll be the new champions," he said. "We'll go twice as far as Heyerdahl with a smaller raft and a smaller crew."

"Let's not brag too soon," Marc warned. "From now on there'll be hurricanes, sharks, and all those damned reefs."

He should have mentioned the boredom and personal tensions, for they would ultimately prove as dangerous as any storm. It was almost inevitable that we would become restless and edgy repeating the same monotonous routine day after day. Yet the very monotony provided an opportunity for reflection, for there is no greater goad to introspection than a long sea voyage. Perhaps it's the mesmeric movement of the waves, the constant ebb and flow, that carries one back to an earlier time, that sometimes forces one to relive and reappraise some painful moments.

My own thoughts were often a jumble of childhood impressions mixed with adult episodes: a teacher slapping my hand and Salvador Dali refusing to shake it; my father clearing phlegm from his throat at three in the morning and the parrot Lorita suddenly dying with a hideous rasping noise tearing from her throat; confessing to an old priest sins I hadn't committed (just in case I should forget some I *had* committed) and telling my wife I had a doctor's appointment to avoid a confrontation with her mother—a ceaseless montage of frustration, fear, and evasion. Then I would run the film over again, editing it here and there so that I might appear in a more positive light.

Then there were days when nothing seemed to go well, when we all felt like prisoners in a floating cell block. The *craack* and *raasp* of Gabriel's spoon was more grating than usual, and even Normand's quiet nature made me edgy. On such days we stayed clear of each other, consciously expanding our "bubbles of privacy." The only one on board who had no sense of privacy was Minet.

One afternoon, as I was sitting near the stern, worrying about my two daughters and feeling guilty for having left them for perhaps six months or more, Minet jumped from the cabin roof and landed on my shoulder.

"Get away!" I snapped, pushing him off. "Leave me alone. I'm not in the mood, you silly cat."

But he persisted, jumping onto my knee and stubbornly hanging on when I tried to pull him off. He seemed suddenly frightened and determined not to be rejected. There were times—and this was one of them—when he was more like a helpless puppy than an ornery independent kitten. Though I'm certain no puppy, or even a full-grown dog, could have survived on *La Balsa* more than three or four days without falling overboard, or getting slapped or bitten by one of the many sharks we dragged on board.

But then Minet, we all agreed, was no ordinary cat. Quite aside from his natural feline endowments (I've been

110

told that the chambers of the brain relating to balance and mobility are unusually large in cats), he probably benefited from his constant diet of raw fish. The rest of us sometimes ate our fish raw but generally preferred to cook it in our small primus stove, which was lashed to a crossbeam in front of the cabin. We had been unable to find the kinds of dried fish and meat the Inca and Huancavilca sailors had eaten, and Gabriel particularly regretted our inability to duplicate their diets.

"We should have stored our drinking water the way the Indians did," I told him. "They used thick bamboo canes. They plugged all the knots in the middle and poured fresh water through a little hole at one end. Then they would use resin as a stopper."

I explained how they stored thirty or forty of these bamboo water tubes in the triangular crevices between the logs, under the matted deck, where they would be protected from the sun and cooled by constant dousing in sea water.

"Why didn't you tell us about this before we left Guayaquil?" asked Marc.

"I considered it," I said. "But I assumed we could carry more water in the jugs, and a lot easier."

"Not really," said Gabriel. "I was figuring it out in my head. If you take a bamboo cane with a four-inch hollow space—and say it's twenty feet long—you've got a lot more volume than any jug we brought along. And you could also carry bamboos *under* the raft."

"Those Indians were pretty smart," said Marc, lifting the woven deck mat as if to calculate how much water could fit in the open spaces. He later told me our water supplies would probably run out before we reached Australia. "Then we'll have to chew raw fish to quench our thirst," he added.

My own reading about the Huancavilcas and Incas had reassured me on this point. Aside from chewing raw fish, they could squeeze the moisture from pieces of fish by twisting them in strips of cloth. They would also extract juices from the lymphatic glands of larger fish like dolphins and tunnies. The first time I tried it, the ooze tasted terrible, but the actual percentage of salt was so low, my thirst quickly vanished in spite of the acrid taste.

There was, of course, a definite need for a certain amount of salt in our diet, and Marc provided us with salt tablets which we took on especially hot days, when perspiration drained our bodies of salt. He also occasionally added saltwater to our regular drinking water, using "a martini ratio" of five-to-one.

"This is a lousy cocktail," I complained.

"But you'll never get a hangover," he said, pouring himself a second.

It also discouraged us from drinking too much water on those blistering hot days when the temperature would rise to a hundred and fifteen degrees in the half-shade of the cabin.

Although he drank his full share of Marc's saltwater cocktail, Gabriel screwed up his face after every swallow. "If we had some coca leaves to chew on, this would be easier to take," he said. "That's what the Incas did. They found out that cocaine would kill the taste of anything. If I had known where to find some I would have stashed some away."

"And you might have become addicted," said Marc.

"You old fogies think everything's addictive," answered Gabriel. "Look at all the nonsense you hear about marijuana. Yet some studies show it's less addictive than ordinary tobacco, and less harmful than alcohol."

Drugs, politics, and the Vietnam war were the principal

topics of conversation on board *La Balsa*. Listening to the shortwave radio broadcasts, one couldn't escape the conclusion that the United States was very much alone in that tragic war.

"Why don't they get out?" Gabriel would ask. "They have no business there—and, besides, they can never win that kind of war. Even the Americans themselves are against it. Think of all the kids who have deserted. That never happened before."

"It may not be so easy to pull out," I said. "They might lose face."

"That's an oriental phobia," insisted Gabriel. "Why should a powerful—"

"You're wrong, Gabriel," interjected Marc. "It's a universal trait. No one likes to lose—especially a powerful nation."

As with the drug problem, we never reached a consensus on the Vietnam war, but I guess we generally agreed that the U.S. was sorry it ever got involved.

Once in a while we discussed some of the books we'd brought with us: *Dog Years*, by ·Günter Grass, *Report to Greco*, by Nikos Kazantzakis, *Le Mur* and *La Nausée* by Jean-Paul Sartre, the letters of Madame de Sevigne, and several science fiction novels. Since our common language was French, we naturally got into some intellectual nitpicking. But when our talk got too serious and semantically involved, Normand would start singing the chorus of a song he had picked up somewhere. He only knew a few words of it, but he kept repeating them over and over.

"He sings better in the bath," Marc observed one morning as Normand lay spread-eagled on the rear deck with the waves washing over him.

We all took baths that way, spreading our arms and legs, and grabbing a rope looped around a crossbeam to keep from being swept off the raft by a backlash. The salt water was cool and refreshing, but our bodies were always left with a powdery residue of salt after we had dried ourselves in the broiling sun.

Gabriel was bothered more than any of us by the itchy salt. "The first thing I'm going to do in Australia is take a long hot shower to get rid of this damned salt," he said, scratching his back. "And then I'm going to eat the biggest meal I've ever eaten."

For some strange reason, he had developed a great fear of starvation. Every morning he would ask Marc about our food supplies.

"We're doing all right," Marc would say.

"Are you sure?" Gabriel would ask.

"Of course. Even if all our rice and canned foods are used up, we still have all the fresh fish we can eat."

"But what if they should disappear if we hit another dead spot in the sea? Then we'd really starve or die of thirst."

He had mentioned the possibility of starvation several times, jokingly at first, then with a certain obsessive anxiety. To allay his fears, I told him we could eat plankton if worse came to worse. I had read about the nutritive value of plankton and algae in a book called *Challenge of Man's Future* by Harrison Brown. Plankton, I learned, is a general name applied to a vast portion of marine life, ranging in size from microorganisms to jellyfish, which drifts along with the sea currents, as distinguished from those organisms (nekton) which can swim and migrate freely, such as fish and squid, and those (benthos) which live on the sea floor, such as sponges, crabs, and clams.

Fortunately, we never reached the point of having to eat plankton, but we did manage to collect some in a cone-shaped cloth suspended from the bow so as to trap the minute organisms drifting toward us.

"Aach! It looks like a mess of fat slimy germs," said Gabriel. "I'd rather starve than eat that stuff."

"Don't worry, Gabriel," said Marc, nudging me. "I'll make us a nice casserole with it—with a fine wine sauce that will make it taste like a French delicacy."

Plankton, seaweed, barnacles, and crabs gradually accumulated on the bottom and sides of *La Balsa,* clinging to the logs like a ragged army of parasites. Determined to get a close-up view of this phenomenon, Gabriel had briefly explored the underside of the raft three or four times, with Normand and Marc keeping a sharp lookout for sharks.

"We've got a botanical garden down there!" he exclaimed.

On his fourth inspection, about three or four hundred miles beyond the Tahitian Islands, he told us that the garden had become a jungle, with thick long strands of seaweed dangling from every log and a bewildering array of sea animals crawling all over. Like creeping ivy, it threatened to climb onto the top deck, around the sides, and between the logs, but we managed to keep it under control by scraping it off periodically. We had less success combating legions of small ants that fed on the seaweed and larvae that got above the water line. In spite of all our precautions, the ants had hidden inside the porous balsa logs before we left Guayaquil, surfacing when we were out at sea.

115

I later learned that insects are often found thousands of miles from their natural habitat, far out on the high seas. On his world-wide voyage aboard the H.M.S. *Beagle,* Charles Darwin found hundreds of small spiders crawling over the rigging when the ship was hundreds of miles off the South American coast. He theorized that they were blown out to sea by the offshore winds, but I think it's more likely that the spiders were simply stowaways that eventually surfaced from their hiding places in fruit crates, bales of cotton, or any other cargo.

"These damned ants will cause us more trouble than an army of sharks," Marc warned when he saw the first few crawling around the stern.

He wasn't far wrong. They swarmed all over the raft, burrowing into our sleeping bags and keeping us awake with mean little stings. They tormented us day and night, creeping up our legs and arms as we sat on deck during the day, sharing our food at every meal.

"Don't these ants ever sleep?" asked Gabriel, scraping one off his breakfast plate.

"In shifts," said Marc. "The morning shift has just come on."

Fortunately, none of them were the poisonous variety we had come across in the jungle forest of Ecuador.

Our best weapon against the ants was provided by nature. During a good heavy storm some of them would be washed overboard—but of course we were also susceptible to the same danger. One such storm struck us early in August. I was lying face down on the rear deck, taking a saltwater bath, when I got the first signal of impending trouble. A huge wave, far heavier than the previous ones, splashed over my body and nearly made me lose hold of the safety strap.

Another hit me before I could struggle to my feet, and pushed me against the cabin. Ahead, dark ominous clouds were rushing toward us from the east, blotting out the sun, and rumbling along with the harsh driving winds that had already aroused the sea.

"All hands on deck!" I yelled. "Here comes a big one. Tie everything down!"

It wasn't necessary to tell them. Marc and Gabriel had already started their emergency duties, and Normand soon joined them. As the wind howled like a demented demon we started to pull in the sail with all the energy we had. Two or three times Normand was nearly swept overboard as he struggled to fold in the lower flap. Struggling with the sail ropes for almost half an hour as successive waves drenched us, we finally got the sail in. Then, just as we were tying it down, a huge wall of water swept toward us and flung the raft sideways up and over the wave's back, just as it broke, hissing and foaming at the crest. Riding through the welter of churning foam which engulfed us, we felt the sea rolling beneath. The bow slanted upward as the first wave passed, then dipped again as we slid down the broad trough. Then the next wall of water came at us, tossing us into the air, carrying us through another curtain of foam and letting us slide down the wave's receding back, tossing us about like a cork.

"Here comes another!" shouted Marc, grabbing the mast with both arms.

"Ooooh b—," I heard Normand say as a deafening clap of thunder drowned out his voice.

A sheet of rain washed over us like a fire hose, slashing the deck and cabin for ten or fifteen minutes. Holding onto the mast, wondering if our bamboo cabin could withstand

117

the vicious onslaught of winds, waves, and heavy rains, I looked up at the dark clouds and began to shout "Chisco!" my nickname for my favorite saint, San Francisco. "Listen to me, Chisco!" I yelled. "Why did you doublecross us this way? Why didn't you give us fair warning?"

But the gale only assaulted us with increased fury, causing the raft to pitch and reel like a mad drunkard. Somehow *La Balsa* managed to withstand the onslaught as wave after wave sent blinding geysers across the deck. Then suddenly, as if an unseen celestial referee had blown a whistle, the storm eased and the raft started riding the waves like a gull.

An hour or so later Gabriel approached me with a serious expression. "You shouldn't have talked that way to Saint Francis," he said, fingering his good luck coin. "It wasn't his fault. After all, you can't expect him to warn us of every summer storm."

It would have been difficult for me to explain that my presumed blasphemy was actually a convenient mask for a deeply felt belief in a Supreme Being. Chisco was merely his surrogate. I rather suspect that most sailors—even those who pride themselves on being tough, hard-drinking womanizers —have a streak of hidden piety in them. Facing the most fundamental elements of nature day after day, they must inevitably come to question the reasons behind such gigantic forces. For the sophisticated landlubber, such phenomena probably can be explained in the abstract logic of a weatherman on a television newscast. They are simply lines on a map, accompanied by a few numbers and a catch phrase or two like "moving storm center" or "slowly developing cold front."

But there are no words, no logic, that can adequately explain the inutterable fury of a screeching wind on a midnight sea. Nor can any poet or painter adequately depict the all-enveloping beauty of a sunset that emblazes the entire horizon or the simple grandeur of the sea itself. For the ordinary seaman—as for me—there must be other ways to explain or convey the mystery of such awesome phenomena. And for those of us who have been raised to believe in the existence of a Superior Being, we generally come to the conclusion that such a Being somehow controls the colossal natural forces that play with our lives in such direct ways.

I also realize, however, that man must help himself all he can, that most prayers for help must seem like insults to a Supreme Being who can't possibly be expected to bother with this man's gout and that woman's obesity—or, for that matter, to guide a raft safely through a storm or a maze of reefs. Not even a surrogate like Saint Francis can be bothered with such trifles.

On the other hand, most of us have been educated to feel we must be afraid of God, and I think this is wrong. No one is small before God. I believe you can speak to him directly and honestly. There were many times at sea when I cursed him, when I shook my fist and asked him why he didn't make the wind stop. I challenged him to come down on the raft with us—to feel the fury of the winds and sea as we felt it. But even then, I did not beg him.

Actually, I think the most we can ask of God is for faith in our better selves and for a renewed belief in the essential fairness of Nature. Having such convictions, I have found it much easier to deal with elemental forces in a straightforward manner—particularly on the high seas.

8

Both the winds and the currents were sluggish during the rest of that first week in August, but we somehow managed to progress another eleven degrees to the west, a snail's pace that would have been doubled had we been favored with decent westerly winds. The listless water was coated with algaeic scum, floating seaweed, and a curious assortment of man-made debris—beer cans, paper plates, and even a bamboo cane with a white plastic handle. Fortunately, a stiff wind soon pushed us away from this ecological grave.

On the afternoon of August 8, as we were moving out of the Polynesian longitudes toward Melanesia, we had a staticky shortwave radio conversation with Rafael Corcuera in Guadalajara, Mexico. Rafael was one of our most faithful supporters and always showed a deep concern for our safety and well-being. Just before we signed off he inevitably asked about our food supplies.

"Gabriel thinks we're going to starve," I said with a chuckle. "And I'm dying for a good steak and some French fries—but Marc says we'll have to eat raw fish for the next two months."

Several days later I learned that we had a terribly faulty circuit, and all Rafael had heard were the words "starve," "dying," and "raw fish." My telltale chuckle hadn't registered at all.

Fearing the very worst, our friend immediately alerted several other ham operators and put in an emergency call to Admiral Fernandez in Mexico City.

"They're dying of starvation," he told him. "We've got to send a rescue ship."

"I'll try to reach them first," the admiral said. "Let's make sure."

Unfortunately, neither of them could make contact with us, since our radio had been getting weaker and weaker as we moved westward. All we could hear were occasional spurts of static and high whining sounds.

"We'd better give this thing a rest," I told Marc shortly after my broken conversation with Corcuera. "Maybe we'll do better in a day or two."

On the second day we had another sputtering talk with Rafael and I thought I heard him ask if we needed a ship, to which I responded with a loud firm "No," which he either didn't hear or chose to ignore.

Meanwhile, I later learned, Corcuera and Fernandez had been in contact with the U.S. Naval Station at Pearl Harbor, telling them that a raft was in distress somewhere between the Polynesian and Melanesian Islands. On the morning of August 11, as we were enjoying a breakfast of flying fish expertly prepared by Marc, we had another frantic and staticky message from Guadalajara informing us that "a ship is on the way." I tried to tell Rafael to leave us alone, but our transmitter was apparently dead.

"Why in God's name does he want to send a ship?" I asked, feeling angry and frustrated.

"Don't let it bother you, Vital," said Marc. "Rafael means well. He's just a worrywart."

No one seemed to share my determination to remain totally independent. "We can't afford any delays," I insisted.

"But you can't ignore another ship," said Marc, rubbing his jaw with the back of his hand. "Maybe their crew is just curious about a raft getting this far."

Sensing a possible personal advantage, Gabriel sided with Marc. "I don't see any harm in meeting them," he said. "Maybe one of them will mail some letters for me."

Normand indicated his preference with an enthusiastic "*Voilà,*" and since I was a minority of one, I eased up a bit. "We'll have to play it by ear, I guess."

"Okay," Marc agreed. "Now let's have a little contest. Whoever sees the ship first will get an extra ten thousand points on his canasta score."

We had been playing a continuous day-to-day game of canasta since our departure from Guayaquil, and most of our scores now exceeded the million mark. The cards, needless to say, showed signs of considerable wear and tear.

"Can we make it twenty thousand points?" asked Gabriel, whose score was less than eight hundred thousand on that particular day.

"All right," said Marc. "Now let's try to think of a gift to give the captain. That's an old maritime custom."

"But what can we possibly give him?" I asked. Not knowing the nationality of the ship or what language the captain spoke, we rejected the idea of presenting him with one of our weatherbeaten books, but we had little else aboard to offer.

"How about some fresh fish?" Gabriel suggested. "Maybe he'd like a dolphin—or a live octopus."

By a vote of three to one, we decided on a dolphin, with Gabriel protesting that he would catch a baby octopus as an extra gift. But none of us could catch anything that morning, not even a sardine. As we were lamenting our bad luck, Normand sighted a small speck to the northeast on the horizon.

"There's the ship," he said, obviously thinking of the twenty thousand points he had just won.

As the speck grew larger, we could see it was a good-sized naval ship. Still several miles away, it managed to establish radio contact with us, and at exactly 5:32 P.M., we heard a voice speaking English:

"You are on our radar," it said. "Only ten miles away. We will be there in an hour."

From the accent I could tell he was an American, and as the ship drew closer we were informed it was the U.S.S. *Hall,* later identified as a "special project and research ship weighing 11,600 tons."

The voice repeated, "You are still on our radar," and I assumed that we were still not visible to them at five or six miles distance. Thinking of the space modules they generally picked up, I could well imagine how primitive our raft would look to them by comparison. As the gray ship got bigger and bigger, cruising straight at us at a gradually diminishing speed, Marc, Normand, and Gabriel stood near the

123

bow, waving, while I remained near the cabin, my ears cocked for further messages on the radio.

When the ship got within a mile of us, it stopped, and a large motor launch was lowered down the starboard side. It roared toward *La Balsa* at a fast clip, spewing a V-shaped froth of white foam.

Less than three minutes later it pulled alongside the raft, and two of the crewmen came on board. They were wearing white T-shirts and pants, which contrasted sharply with our ragged and bleached denim shorts and darkly tanned bodies. They greeted us warmly and told us that the captain had invited us to dinner on board the ship.

"We do not want to trouble you," I answered in my halting, heavily accented English. "You are too kind."

They smiled and shook their heads, saying, "No trouble at all. Everyone wants to meet you."

With no further ado, they attached a tow rope to our bow and started tugging *La Balsa* toward the ship. Meanwhile I went back to the cabin to answer a signal on our radio, which seemed to be working better now. It was Joe Megan calling from Guayaquil.

"Vital!" he exclaimed, through the static. "I can't believe this, amigo. I've been in touch with an American ship that's close to you, the U.S.S. *Hall*. They say you're west of the Polynesian longitudes, far beyond the landing of *Kon-Tiki!*"

"Of course," I said. "I reported that several days ago."

"Yes, I know," he said. "But when I kept getting your reports on that lousy radio I fixed for you, I thought you were pulling some kind of joke on everybody. I didn't believe you could transmit messages from anywhere beyond the Galapagos."

"Well, I'm not a liar," I said, perhaps too testily.

Then another voice broke into our circuit, the low resonant voice of Admiral Fernandez from Mexico City. "I've always believed in you, Vital. Congratulations and a warm embrace."

I was so absorbed in my radio conversation with Megan and Fernandez that I failed to notice a commotion outside the cabin. Then I heard a tremendous jolt, followed by a crunching noise, and, rushing to the deck, I saw the huge gray bulk of the U.S.S. *Hall* looming over us. The motor launch had pulled us too close to the ship, and an undertow (probably created by the rocking of the ship's bow) was dragging us against the hull. Fearing it would crush the raft, Marc and Gabriel had grabbed some bamboo poles and were desperately trying to push away from the ship. Normand's pole had already broken and he was looking for another.

"Why didn't you call me?" I yelled, grabbing the swinging boom and pulling it away from the ship as it tilted toward us again.

"Watch out!" someone cried, as the hull rammed us again with a loud splintering crunch.

"Our trip is over," I said to myself with a sick feeling in my guts. "The raft will be smashed to pieces."

Pushing the bamboo poles against the hull with all our might, cursing and praying, we made a last desperate effort to save the raft, somehow managing to shove it away as the ship rocked toward us again. The four of us were braced on the starboard log, our bamboo poles held ready for the next assault, when suddenly the ship moved away from us. The captain had obviously seen our danger and given the order to pull away—gradually, however, so as not to increase the undertow. Once we were clear, the ship's crew gave out a cheer, yelling *bravo!* and *olé!* at the top of their lungs.

Once again the motor launch pulled alongside the raft

and picked us up for the short trip back to the ship. But Minet wouldn't come with us. Frightened by the strangers (or was it the monstrous ship?), he squirmed out of Gabriel's arms, his fur bristling as he scampered into our cabin.

"I guess he doesn't like us," said one of the young Americans, looking slightly hurt.

"He's scared of the ship," I remarked. "He's never seen anything bigger than the raft."

"Maybe the noise scared him," he replied, surveying the raft. "We heard something crack down here."

"That was only the toilet," I said, attempting to conceal my disappointment as I pointed to the mess of crushed and splintered balsa wood on the starboard log that had been our head.

"Hey, guys," he yelled to his mates. "They had an outdoor john, and we busted it. "I'm awful sorry, sir. That's a damned shame."

"Could be worse," I said with a grin.

Waving goodbye to Minet, who was standing at the cabin doorway with an aloof, go-ahead-and-leave-me expression, we jumped into the launch and hurried toward the waiting ship.

The reception we got was tremendous. The entire crew huddled around us as we came aboard, shaking our hands, patting our shoulders, congratulating us, and asking a hundred questions about *La Balsa*. On the fringe of this exuberant crowd, patiently waiting for his men to finish their initial greetings, was the captain himself, W. P. Karmenzid. Finally someone cleared a path for him and he stepped forward to shake hands with each of us, a smile lighting his bronzed finely chiseled face.

"Welcome aboard," he said in a resonant voice. "Our

ship is yours. And please forgive us for the damage we caused. We were terribly clumsy."

"No damage to mention," I said, again in my best Berlitz English. "You are kind to invite us."

I then introduced myself and my crew; and he introduced the officers of his crew, escorting us to the officers' quarters.

"You must be tired and hungry," he said. "We were told that you've run out of food—that you're nearly starving."

I stopped in my tracks, scarcely believing my ears. "Who told you this?" I exclaimed.

"Señor Corcuera, the man from Guadalajara. He called us on the shortwave radio," said the captain. "We got the first alert from our command in Pearl Harbor two days ago."

I was flabbergasted. "I don't understand," I mumbled. "We eat very well. Plenty of fish all the time. How could Rafael say we are starving?"

Then as I suddenly remembered my conversation with Rafael and the heavy static that apparently fractured each sentence, I began to smile. "Poor Corcuera," I said to Captain Karmenzid. "He didn't realize I was making a joke. I said to him, 'Gabriel always thinks we are going to starve. And I'm dying for a good steak and French fries.' But the connection was so bad he must have only caught bits and pieces."

The captain was smiling now, so were his three officers, as I emphasized the words "going to starve" and "dying."

"No wonder he started to worry," said Karmenzid. "I'll bet those were the only words he heard. And then your radio went dead, and he couldn't contact you. We also tried to contact you, since yesterday, but couldn't get through until this afternoon."

When I explained the misunderstanding to Marc, Normand, and Gabriel, speaking to them in French, they laughed as I repeated the crucial words which had probably agitated Rafael.

"Well, even if there is no emergency," said the captain, "We're glad you're here, Captain Alsar. And you can stay as long as you wish."

Though we appreciated the offer, I told him we could only stay an hour or so, that we had a jealous and angry cat waiting for us. But we gladly accepted and hungrily devoured a fine dinner of steaks, French fries, creamed asparagus, marinated beets, hot biscuits with real butter, apple pie, and ice cream. No one ever had a more delightful banquet. "We must be eating like sharks," I remarked somewhat apologetically, accepting a second serving of pie.

"You're welcome to everything we have," said the first mate in a soft Southern drawl.

Judging from what was to follow, he apparently meant every word. When we boarded the launch an hour and a half later, there were several crates and boxes of canned food and a metal container of gasoline for our radio generator. "We brought a few things for you," said the mate. "With the captain's compliments." He also told us that Karmenzid was an American Indian from the Navajo tribe, and he showed great pride in serving under him.

What a marvelous coincidence: here in the mid-Pacific a giant modern naval vessel directed by an American Indian had encountered a small raft fashioned like the balsa rafts that were used perhaps three thousand years ago by Indians who might have been indirectly related to his ancestors.

When we got back to *La Balsa,* Minet was waiting for us on the cabin roof like a haughty gargoyle. He sat there, scarcely twitching a muscle, as we scrambled from the launch onto the raft, and remained silent and aloof while we helped the *Americanos* unload the supplies they had given us, thanking them again and again.

"These Americans are incredible!" said Gabriel, as he hauled in a large box of canned fruit. "No one is more generous than them. They have the souls of children."

Recalling his previous statements about "money-grubbing materialistic gringos," I answered with a restrained smile. "Yes, Gabriel, they have that reputation."

But when the motor launch and the U.S.S. *Hall* had disappeared into the darkening horizon, I asked my crew to help me dispose of the supplies. "We'll have to dump it overboard, *amigos,*" I said. "They're gone now, so they won't see us."

Gabriel was absolutely dumbfounded. "But why?" he asked.

"Because we have to make it on our own," said Marc.

"It's also too heavy and cumbersome," I added. "All these boxes will get in the way. We have to keep traveling light, Gabriel."

Reluctantly, with a hungering look at each separate box, he helped us dump our American bounty into the sea —though he did manage to salvage a few cans of peaches and pineapple, persuading us that they weren't enough to vitiate our theory of self-survival. Marc also saved a can of steaks. "This label says it was packed ten years ago, and I'm curious to see how well it's been preserved."

Actually, it was better than we had anticipated—not exactly great, but certainly adequate.

Buoyed by this repast, Gabriel managed to set aside his worries about starving to death—but not for long. Three or four days after our meeting with the U.S.S. *Hall,* as we were approaching a passage between the islands of Tongareva and Vostok, he sat alongside me on the crossbeam near the bow, his eyes squinting at the lowering sun.

"We shouldn't have thrown away that food," he said without preface. "I think we're going to need it."

I tried to make light of his worries though I knew they were genuine. "But we have all kinds of fish, Gabriel—look out there."

"Not as many as yesterday," he persisted. "The wind is going down, and the current's slowing. I think we're headed for another dead spot."

I tried to persuade him that the winds and currents were never constant. "This calm could break at any moment, maybe tonight."

He seemed not to hear me, his blue-gray eyes staring beyond me, his jaw muscles twitching lightly as he tightened his chapped lips. Listening to his worried warnings about starvation, I was suddenly reminded of the famous Donner party that got trapped in a snowstorm in the High Sierras and finally succumbed to cannibalism when they began starving to death. Looking around at Marc and Normand, I wondered if we, too, would be capable of such a thing under similar circumstances. When do we reach the limits of civilized conduct? When does a friend or even a brother become expendable, a necessary sacrifice to one's own survival?

Sitting there in the immense loneliness of the Pacific, knowing that it *was* possible to starve if we were stranded on a lifeless, fishless sea, I tried to visualize myself eating the flesh of one of my companions—and I finally decided it would be impossible, that I would rather starve. Yet I had to concede that I had never reached a state of impending starvation, when a man's psyche must surely change, so how could I (or anyone) be sure?

Gabriel suddenly broke into my morbid speculation. "We could be stuck for several days without moving an inch."

"No, Gabriel," said Marc. "We can always row. That's what the oars are for—to get us moving again till we find another current."

Not entirely persuaded, he nodded his head and gave a dubious smile. "Well, at least Minet won't starve," he said. "He'll eat anything, even that lousy plankton."

We had been watching Minet play a new game. He was standing in a crouched position on the portside log, his right paw batting at the water, as if he were punching invisible flies or teasing a fish.

"He's leaning out too far," said Gabriel. "I'm going to pull him back."

Just then, Minet snapped out his paw and lost his balance, splashing into the water with a loud meow! Rushing toward him, Gabriel tripped on the loose edge of the deck mat and plopped on his belly. Stunned for a moment, he got up again and reached the edge of the raft just as I did.

"My God!" he called. "Look at that!"

Minet had surfaced and was now swimming back to the raft, paddling with his forepaws and meowing furiously as we plunked him out of the water.

"He swam at least five feet!" I exclaimed.

"More," insisted Gabriel, cuddling the drenched and shivering cat in his arms. "It was at least six feet."

By now Normand and Marc had joined us, laughing

with pride as we told them what had happened. Realizing he was the object of considerable adulation, Minet lifted his head and shook off the water with a charming arrogance.

"Now that we know this cat can actually swim," I suggested, "we must give him some more lessons. Starting tomorrow."

"You're crazy, Vital," said Gabriel. "He'll drown."

"He may have to swim some day to save his life," I said. "Especially through the rough seas we're expecting. All I'm trying to do is give him some practice, so he won't panic if he should get thrown overboard."

They argued against me all evening but eventually conceded that it might be necessary to prepare for such an emergency.

The first lesson began right after my morning watch. With Normand and Gabriel poised on the starboard log like short-distance swimming champions, I grabbed Minet around his stomach, whispered a word of encouragement to him, and gently tossed him into the water six to seven feet away from the raft. Almost instantly he bobbed up and pivoted to face the raft, meowing angrily, then started swimming toward us. It took him less than fifteen seconds to cover the distance.

"Bravo, gatito!" said Gabriel, reaching out to pull him in.

A few minutes later, I tossed him about twelve feet out, and once again he started paddling back to us, his strokes more measured and regular than before. This time, when Normand scooped him out of the water, he eyed us with cool hauteur, accepting our praise like a seasoned champion, strutting around the deck with his tail raised straight up in the air.

132

We repeated the experiment twice more that day, rowing him out to twenty feet, then thirty feet. "He'll go even farther tomorrow," I said, drying him off with my shirt.

Once again my crewmates protested.

"We know the cat can swim enough to save himself. He doesn't need more practice."

But I was still determined to extend the distance, to test the outer limits of his survival power. So after lunch the next day, while the others sprawled out on the rear mat for a short siesta, I got into the dinghy with Minet and started rowing away from the raft before they could object. Gabriel spotted me when I was about ten feet away.

"Vital!" he yelled. "What are you doing with Minet? You promised—"

"I promised nothing," I said with a grin.

There was anger and frustration in Gabriel's voice as he was joined at the bow by Marc and Normand. "He's double-crossed us," he told them. "He promised to stop—he's going to drown that cat!"

I kept on rowing, whispering encouragement in Minet's ear as he sat on the edge of the rubber boat with cool assurance. Finally, when I had reached a point fifty or sixty feet from the raft, I put aside the oars.

"Don't!" shouted Gabriel. "He'll drown, Vital," called Marc.

Ignoring their protests, I shoved the cat toward the raft, saying *"Buena suerte."*

Without the slightest hesitation, he started paddling with his tiny white forepaws, meowing softly to himself like a coxswain calling the pace for a long row. He started so well that I immediately felt a sense of relief. So, apparently, did Normand, Gabriel, and Marc, who were leaning forward at the bow and watching every stroke of his progress as if he were a baby taking his first steps.

Then abruptly Minet paused in mid-stroke. Thrashing the water for a second or two, he let out a loud meow! and started back to the dinghy, paddling furiously. With my oar already in the water, I surged toward him with two desperate strokes, as I spotted a six-foot shark racing toward us. Lunging forward, nearly capsizing the dinghy, I grabbed Minet out of the water as the shark closed in with its toothy mouth wide open and ready to snap shut. It missed Minet by less than two feet as it swished past us. Then, ten or twelve feet beyond the dinghy, it made a U-turn and came back at us, dipping under and around us as I rowed toward the raft with Minet snuggled on my lap. Every now and then he would stretch forward for a closer look at the pursuing shark, and once or twice I felt him flinch as it snapped at my oar.

"Don't worry, Minet," I assured him. "If he takes my oar, Marc will tow us in with a rope."

Apparently anticipating that possibility, Marc was standing ready near the bow, holding a coiled rope. But there was no need to use it. The shark snared the oar twice but I twisted it away, and he finally dived out of sight as Minet and I boarded the raft.

"I'm sorry," I said, feeling guilty and foolish. "That was really stupid of me."

"It's okay," said Gabriel in a reassuring voice that no doubt required restraint. "Minet learned something from this. He got exposed to the worst danger—and survived."

To celebrate, Marc cooked a fine dinner of tuna stuffed with tenderized barnacles and finely chopped seaweed, and later distributed our weekly ration of cigarettes. He informed us that he had reduced the ration by one-half, and with a previous reduction a month earlier, we were now smoking one-fourth as much as we did on our first month out of Guayaquil. I didn't mind the reduction, but I had detected a certain change in Marc's behavior. He was becoming short-tempered and occasionally sulked about minor irritations. Knowing he had been a habitual chain-smoker, I frequently gave him some of my own cigarettes. Even so, I would sometimes catch him scavenging around the deck for Normand's one-inch butts, carefully unwrapping the lip-wet paper and depositing the remaining tobacco into a small red can. Clearly, this called for a sacrifice from those of us who were not so addicted.

At the first opportunity, when Marc was on night watch, I conferred with Gabriel and Normand. "This tobacco shortage is too much for him," I said. "He's liable to blow his stack."

"He might," agreed Gabriel. "He's got a big hangup on that stuff. With me, it doesn't matter, but he's really hurting."

"Well, as far as I'm concerned," I said. "He can have all my cigarettes starting tomorrow."

"That's okay by me," said Gabriel. "He's got mine, too."

We looked at Normand, who had remained silent as usual, not knowing how we would react since he was probably fonder of tobacco than either of us.

"Okay," he finally said, stroking his scraggy beard. "Marc needs it more."

"Ooooh boooy!" exclaimed Gabriel, winking at me. "C'est formidable."

9

At noon on August 25, I took a sextant reading and found that we were passing the meridian of 160 degrees—two-thirds of the way toward our goal. On this trackless, signless sea, it was just another invisible milestone, but to us it had special, almost metaphysical significance. We were beating the odds, doing what everyone had thought was impossible.

"This calls for a celebration," said Marc. "I've saved something for this occasion, it's under the mat behind the cabin."

We crowded around him as he lifted the bamboo mat and pulled out an object wrapped in several layers of banana leaves. It was a bottle of champagne that he had brought from Montreal. "There's another one," he said. "For the day we reach Australia."

Normand produced some yellow plastic cups, and we drank a toast to *La Balsa*.

Several hours later, I decided it was time for another thorough inspection of the logs. Bearing in mind we had already traveled nearly six thousand miles, I was particularly concerned about the possible absorption of water through the grooves we had made for the ropes.

With my feet braced under a crossbeam, I leaned over the portside log and studied a rope groove near the middle just below the water level. It was soft and foam-rubbery around the edges, swollen like kissed lips. Firmly pressing it with my thumb, I felt it yield for a half inch, water oozing and bubbling from the cut edge; and then it stiffened, resisting further pressure. Not bad, I thought. But wanting to make sure, I carefully punctured it with an ice pick, twisting it slightly when it was about a half inch deep. Pulling it out again, I held it up for a closer view of several tiny particles of balsa wood. They looked dry—fluffy white and dry as sawdust.

"*Voilà!*" I said to Marc, showing him the minute samples. "It's still dry inside."

A quick but careful check of the other six logs yielded the same results: the water penetration had been minimal. Also, we were happy to note that we had lost less than an inch in water level. We next checked the ropes and found them in equally good condition. There was hardly any erosion or splitting, and most of the knots were tighter than ever.

The affirmative diagnosis of *La Balsa's* health gave our morale a considerable boost. We sang more, joked more, ate more, and played more canasta. Even the winds and currents seemed more favorable, propelling us in a southwesterly

137

direction at an average of 130 miles a day. The islands of Samoa were not far off, prompting Gabriel to speculate about the women we might see.

Pursuing this train of thought, he suggested that we try to contact Liliana on the radio and listen to her lovely voice. An hour later, after considerable fiddling with our patched-up transceiver, we heard the melodic sweetness of Liliana's voice.

"We'll soon be in Pago-Pago," whispered Gabriel, "where they have the most fantastic women in the world. But they're only for Normand and me. You old married men will have to stay on the raft."

He talked on about the women he would meet in Samoa, pausing only when Liliana's voice would break through the shrill crackling static, describing in detail how he would teach them to sing Chilean love ballads, to dance the *cuenca,* to say "I love you" in French, Spanish, German, and Greek, and to comb his beard and scratch his salt-powdered back where it itched the most.

Suddenly the radio went completely dead, and Gabriel stopped his tantalizing spiel in mid-sentence. "Hey! We got cut off!"

"This damned machine," I said, slapping the bottom of the radio. "Something snapped inside."

For several hours Marc and I tried to repair it, dismantling the coils, tubes, dials, interconnections, and what-not, spreading them out on the rear deck, hoping they wouldn't be jumbled by a sudden lurch of the raft, the sea having gotten increasingly rough. We finally reassembled the parts by lamplight, but it still wouldn't work.

"Joe Megan was right after all," I said. "It couldn't work forever. We'll have to finish the trip without it."

The next day I took it apart again, shaving and retwisting the ends of the receiver coils, scraping rust from the dial fittings and putting them all together again. Still dead. Not even a trace of static.

On the third day Gabriel took over, methodically tightening every screw on the radio, periodically spanking the top and sides with a few coaxing phrases in Spanish and French. Suddenly the set responded with a low whining noise.

"It works!" shouted Gabriel. "Listen to that beautiful static."

A few moments later we heard the half-garbled voice of Admiral Fernandez, from Mexico City. "Are you listening, are you listening?" he kept saying. "We've been trying to contact you for two days. Your voice was cut off on Wednesday. Now I'm getting a clicking sound from your transmitter."

I shouted into our microphone, but apparently all he heard was the clicking.

"If you hear me," said Fernandez, "disconnect the main transmitter coil and use it like a telegrapher's contact signal."

I followed his instructions, holding the tip of the coil close to the contact screw, waiting for his next order.

"Okay," he said, "apparently you hear me. Now make three long clicks."

"Cliiiiick—cliiiiick—cliiiiick."

"That's fine. Now remember that a long click is 'yes' and two short clicks are 'no.' I'm going to ask you specific questions, and you will answer with clicks. If you still hear me, say 'yes' with a long click."

"Cliiiiick."

139

"Okay, Vital. Now I want to make sure this is really you. I want you to say 'yes' or 'no' to these questions. Do you understand?"

"Cliiiiick."

"You are forty-five years old?"

"Click-click." (No—I was thirty-seven years old.)

"Is your wife's name Denise?"

"Cliiiiick."

"Do you have three sons?"

"Click-click." (No—I have two daughters.)

Having thus verified my identity, Fernandez proceeded to get other, more pertinent information about our progress.

"Concerning your present speed, are you making twenty to thirty miles per day?"

"Click-click."

"Are you going faster?"

"Cliiiiick."

"Are you going more than fifty miles?"

"Cliiiiick."

"More than seventy-five?"

"Cliiiiick."

"More than one hundred?"

"Cliiiiick."

His voice seemed pleased with my answers, but he knew we couldn't be going much faster than a hundred miles per day.

"Are you making a hundred ten to a hundred twenty miles?"

"Click-click."

"Between a hundred twenty and a hundred thirty miles?"

"Cliiiiick."

"Is it about a hundred twenty-five miles per day?"

"Cliiiiick."

Applying the same technique, Fernandez got specific data regarding our longitude, latitude, approximate direction, the speed of the current, the amount of food and water on board, and whether or not any of us were ill. It was a slow painstaking procedure that required great patience on the part of our friend. Going a step further, the admiral promised to contact a ham operator in Australia and teach him our system.

"You will be much closer to him. The signals will be clearer."

I knew, however, that he himself would make every effort to remain the key man in our communications setup. Yet now that our transmitter was virtually dead (we couldn't have managed the full Morse code), our limited radio communications were of greater use to our friends than to us. In any real emergency our slow question-answer method would probably be useless. It would help, nevertheless, to keep the admiral informed of our approximate position.

But our system almost went awry a few days later. Normand usually watched the motor while I operated the radio, taking it outside the cabin so the generator wouldn't interfere with my hearing. On this particular afternoon he was perched on the starboard log with the small motor resting on his lap when a huge wave smashed into us and knocked him overboard. Clutching the motor to his stomach like a fullback, Normand sank into the water in a crouched position, bobbed to the surface, and grabbed a strand of rope on the starboard log with his free hand.

"Get the motor!" he yelled, as Gabriel scrambled across the deck to rescue him.

Bracing himself, Gabriel leaned over and snatched the motor with one hand, pulling Normand aboard with the other.

"That's a great act," I said. "In and out of the water in ten seconds flat."

"We'll charge admission next time," said Gabriel, handing me the drenched motor. "Sorry about breaking the touch rule though," he said jokingly.

"That doesn't apply in emergencies," I said.

It had not been easy to observe our rule of no physical contact, especially at the beginning. We were all *latinos* (a Spaniard, a Chilean, two Frenchman), accustomed to touching people during ordinary conversations, to greeting friends with affectionate *abrazos* whether they were male or female. But we were beginning to acquire a reserve more characteristic of Englishmen. In Shaw's *Don Juan in Hell,* one of the characters says, "The English think they're in love when they're merely comfortable." I began to feel surprisingly "comfortable" in my self-imposed bubble of privacy, deliberately avoiding everyone as I moved about the raft. After a while, the avoidance was no longer deliberate; it became so unconscious that I wondered if I would ever recover my Latin penchant for demonstrative affection.

We all adjusted to this condition of self-restraint, but there were other conditions to which we could never become reconciled. One of the worst was the ants, which seemed to grow more numerous every day and plagued us constantly. There was no place we could go to get away from them, and sometimes I prayed aloud for a hurricane that would wash them away.

"You shouldn't say that," warned Gabriel one afternoon, "your prayers just might be answered."

One evening early in September, as we were approaching the islands of Samoa, the gods apparently decided to respond. The sunset had been startlingly beautiful, an ocher and tangerine splash of color illuminating a vast tumult of clouds slowly drifting across the horizon. The sea itself was like a rippling flame that cast a warm glow over us.

"That's the most fantastic sunset I've ever seen," said Marc, lying near the bow. "No artist could paint that."

But as the sun went down, and the blood-red colors faded, the clouds looked menacing and the water became ominously dark and choppy. Then suddenly the winds came up, whipping our sail around and slashing it against our heads as we hastily pulled it in.

"Grab your ropes," I yelled, as a fifteen-foot wave picked us up and sent us hurtling along on the foamy crest. "Tie yourselves to . . ."

A second wave deluged us before I could finish, but I didn't have to; my crewmates had already secured themselves, and I quickly grabbed a rope to do the same. Before I could reach the mast, however, a huge fifteen-foot wall of water caught us broadside, crashing over the cabin and slamming me to the deck. Dazed and stunned, I managed to scramble to my feet and grabbed the mast as an even larger wave gushed through the cabin doorway and spilled out the windows, carrying a sleeping bag with it.

Unable to see anything in the darkness and driving rain, we were like blind men in a house of horrors, not knowing where the next assault would come from and defenseless even if we had. As wave after wave hit us and furious winds tossed us in all directions, we clung to the mast and crossbeams like frightened crabs and attempted feeble jokes to keep up our courage.

"The gods heard you, Vital," shouted Gabriel. "Three ants went overboard with that last wave."

"They didn't go overboard," I said, between mouthfuls of salt water. "I swallowed them."

Finally, after two hours of relentless punishment, the winds subsided, leaving us numb with exhaustion and drenched to the bone.

"It's too dark to check the damage," said Gabriel, barely visible in the moonless night. "You guys get some sleep. I've got the night watch. Minet will help me."

The next morning we surveyed the results of the storm. The deck and cabin were a shambles, water-soaked debris everywhere—Marc's torn sleeping bag hanging limply from one crossbeam and pages from Gabriel's Chilean songbook plastered against another; my tattered denim shorts flopped over the portable stove as if to protect it, and a shredded red shirt wrapped around the starboard log like a blood-soaked bandage. Our radio cable was tangled around the splintered boom and bamboo splinters jutted from the cabin roof like stubborn cowlicks on a schoolboy. Aft the cabin, thirty or forty half-dead fish squirmed and flopped pathetically as Minet danced between them to soundless music. It was altogether a dispiriting sight.

"It could have been worse," I said, falling back on that timeless cliché.

"I'm afraid it *will* be," cautioned Marc. "We're coming into the cyclone zone."

We had known this all along—Admiral Fernandez had clearly marked the climate changes on our map—but that baptismal night storm was a most emphatic reminder of the dangers we faced ahead. Two more thunder squalls assaulted us before we reached Samoa, neither of them quite as severe as the first one. During a few sunny interludes we tightened the beams of our wobbly cabin, repaired the splintered boom, and washed and dried our sun-faded shirts and pants in the hot tropical sun.

We were down to twelve pieces of laundry: four shirts, four pairs of pants, and four sleeping bags. But since we spent most of the time in the nude, except for loincloths, our clothing needs were minimal.

Depending upon the winds, we expected to go past Samoa either between Tutuila and Upolu, or else along the northern coast of a sixty-mile-long island called Savaii. The latter route was decided for us by night winds coming from the north. At sunrise on September 12, a cloudless balmy morning, we sighted the green-tipped fringe of Savaii—the first land we had seen since passing the Galapagos Islands more than thirteen weeks before.

Climbing to the roof of the cabin for a better view, Marc, Gabriel, and I shouted "Saaamoooaaa! Saaamoooaaa!" while Normand contented himself with a bubbling "oh boooy!"

Through our only pair of binoculars, we could see the far-off spire of a neo-Gothic church surrounded by glittering green palm trees.

"Beautiful girls on that island," Gabriel speculated, pressing the binoculars to his eyes.

"Fully dressed and Christianized," said Marc. "Anyway, you won't see them."

"Why not?"

"Because there's a reef between us and them. We've got to stay clear."

Momentarily dejected, Gabriel looked longingly at the fertile beauty of the island as we glided past the eastern half,

145

then suddenly came alive with hope. "Maybe there's an opening in the reef, a dip somewhere."

"Maybe," I said. "The maps can't show everything."

Visualizing a few willowy girls in bright flowered sarongs dancing on the beach, I focused the lens on the church and several sun-bleached houses nearby, but my imaginary dancers kept impinging on the white walls of the buildings like a movie montage.

Savaii was a continuously tantalizing sight, with tall coconut palms gently bending in the breeze, multicolored birds flitting among the trees, the white-capped surf swelling toward sandy beaches of sun-splashed coves here and there. At midday we were parallel to the church, a jagged reef partially obscuring the lower half. We were then traveling about five miles per hour.

Four hours later the wind changed, carrying us closer to the island, too close to the reef for comfort. We pulled in the sail but still came closer. The wind was from the north now, and we needed a more easterly one to clear the western tip of the island.

"You may get your wish," I told Gabriel, anxiously scanning the surface for some trace of the threatening reef, which now lay submerged like a waiting trap. "I hope there's an opening—low enough and wide enough."

I hoped even more for a stiff wind from the east, or a south wind if necessary, but we got only a north wind, steadily pushing us closer to Savaii. With the binoculars, I spent the next three hours searching the rippling expanse of water for the telltale sign of foamy surf beating against a reef, but the only surf I saw was washing against the distant coastal beaches.

By sunset we were about three miles offshore, still drifting southwest toward the island. Flickering lights and gentle spirals of wood smoke appeared here and there along the shore.

"Smell that cooking," said Gabriel, hungrily leaning in that direction.

"That's only your imagination," said Marc. "The wind is blowing the other way. You're smelling the fish in this pan."

"Why don't we signal them," suggested Gabriel. "Perhaps they'll come out and tell us about the reefs you're worried about, Vital. Maybe there aren't any."

Marc fired two flares, and a half hour later we saw a motor launch coming our way. There were three men on board, a New Zealander and two Samoans, all of whom assured us that the wind would be changing—"in a few hours." One of the natives excitedly told us he had towed Captain William Willis ashore at Savaii in 1964, and asked if we had ever met him.

"I met him in New York a year later," I said.

Just before my ill-fated trip on the *Pacifica,* I had met Captain Willis at the Explorers Club in Manhattan. "You can't do it," he had said when I told him my plans for sailing to Australia. But a little while later, noting my stubbornness, he said, "Maybe—maybe you can, but it won't be easy." After a long lecture on currents, dangerous reefs, and "wicked weather," he sent me to his favorite store to buy charts for my expedition. At the age of seventy-two he himself had drifted to Savaii single-handed in a steel pontoon raft called *Age Unlimited*. Leaving the port of Callao, Peru, on July 4, 1963, he had reached Savaii on November 11, remained there for seven months (during which time his raft was refitted), and embarked again on July 26, 1964, landing near Tully, North Queensland, about three months later. He lost his life four years later while crossing the Atlantic in a sloop, once again sailing alone.

"He was a brave man," I told our visitors.

Having finished our recollection of Captain Willis, I asked the Samoans if they could possibly bring us some fruit.

"It might be too late to go ashore and come back again," said the New Zealander. "Why don't you let us tow you ashore, and you can get all you want."

"We might miss a good wind," I said, not wanting to seem rude and ungrateful. "We're anxious to get going."

"The east wind won't come for a few hours," he reminded me. "This norther will stay on a while. So you may as well come in, Captain. I'm sure these good people would love to see you. They're very kind—and curious."

"How about reefs?" I asked.

"None in this area," he said. "We've got a clean go in Sataua Bay."

So, I thought to myself, the "reefs" I had seen were merely choppy waves, figments of my storm-weary imagination—caution is often its own worst enemy, especially when you're tired.

Yielding to smiling soft-spoken pressure from the Samoans, who kept pointing toward the village lights blinking in the distance, we agreed to go into the bay for an hour or two. We hadn't reckoned on the extent of their hospitality. The moment we pulled into shallow water a laughing arm-thrashing swarm of people climbed onto the raft and snooped into every corner, jiggling the boom, peering into the cabin, touching the still-warm frying pan, stooping down for a close look at the rope grooves on the portside log, frightening Minet into dead silence with their jabber.

"Please! Please!" I yelled to no one in particular. "We're very tired. We have to sleep a little."

We were finally left alone about 3 A.M., more exhausted than if we'd been through a storm. Lying on the deck, with the raft gently rocking under us, I could hear the ropes softly squeaking as the logs shifted ever so slightly. The ropes holding the mast were white as nylon, dried salt reflecting the moonlight.

Taking the night watch, I told Marc we should leave as soon as we got a proper wind. But the early-morning visitors came before the hoped-for winds and brought us piles of fruit and hot native food. After greedily devouring the native dishes, we pulled up the sail, waved goodbye to our friends, and once again continued our journey with a steady wind blowing from the south.

Minet had come out of his hiding place and was playing with some crabs near the stern, faking a hurt meow whenever one of them snapped at his paws. We were so fascinated by his newly developed ham acting, none of us noticed a large hooked-beaked bird hovering over us. (It was, I subsequently learned, a wandering albatross with a wingspread of seven or eight feet and clumsy webbed feet.)

Catching us unawares, it swooped down at a sharp angle, swishing past us like a shadow and grabbing Minet with his beak. Thrown off balance by its squirming prey, the albatross flapped its wings erratically as it tried to continue its flight. When they were about seven feet in the air Minet made a furious twist that forced his kidnapper to drop him just behind the cabin.

"*Asesino!*" screamed Gabriel, running toward Minet, who had, in true cat fashion, landed on his feet. "I'll kill that bird!"

There was a large gash in Minet's neck; a two-inch hunk of fur had been ripped off by the albatross, but he seemed more angry than injured.

"I'm glad he had webbed feet," said Marc, inspecting the wound with expert fingers. "If he had had claws like an eagle or a hawk, Minet would be done for. He was just too heavy for his beak."

"It wasn't his weight. It was Minet's twisting that did it," said Gabriel proudly. "He refused to go. That's a tough cat."

As if he understood, Minet lifted his drooping head and stuck his tail in the air, thereby causing a new spurt of blood from the wound. We wiped it clean with fresh drinking water, ripped an old shirt in strips, and gently wrapped a bandage around his neck. He looked like a clown in the puffy gauze collar, as he strutted near the bow arrogantly surveying his domain.

But soon he was busy trying to tear the bandage off his neck. Within the first few hours he clawed it to shreds, dragging strands of blood-splotched gauze wherever he went, forcing us to replace the collar three times before Marc found a solution.

"Let's put gauze mittens on his paws—to cover those sharp claws," he suggested. "Or that wound will never heal."

So with four puffed paws and a puffy neck, Minet crept around the deck for the next few days like a practiced burglar, occasionally licking one mitten and washing his face and body with the tongue-wet gauze. Somehow, it never occurred to him to rip off the foot bandages with his teeth.

"That would ruin his act," observed Marc when I mentioned it. "Minet is too much of a ham to spoil a good comedy."

We had albatross following us most of the way across, hovering over head, changing color subtly as the sky changed from east to west, becoming lighter the nearer we came to Australia, where the sky takes on a lighter, paler blue. Often an albatross would hitch on with us, staying for a few hours or even a few days, whatever its whim. Usually these stowaways were innocuous enough, but occasionally one or another of us would—like Minet—have reason to rue their presence.

One night, for example, Gabriel was on night watch, when we were awakened by a great commotion. We sat up in the cabin and peered out; it was pitch dark and we could see nothing, so we called out to Gabriel, but there was no answer. Fearing he had fallen overboard, we made for the door. There stood the bearded Chilean completely unruffled.

"What happened?" I asked.

"Nothing."

"But we felt a huge jolt."

"I didn't feel anything," he insisted, glancing away.

Further questioning was to no avail, so we settled back in our sleeping bags, relieved that he was all right. No more was said about the incident, but Gabriel was strangely reserved for the next couple of days. Then, about the third day, as we were all sitting around having our usual game of Parcheesi, he broke his silence.

"You know?" he said apropos of nothing.

"What?" asked Marc.

"That jolt."

We had almost forgotten. "Well, what was it?" asked Marc.

"Well, I was about to settle down on the can . . . it was pitch dark, you know, I couldn't see a damn thing."

"So?"

(We all had a more or less regular routine for using the head, and since there was little privacy, we usually took advantage of the dark nights.)

"Damned albatross must have been sleeping in it, and when I sat down, he bit me right on the ass!"

We howled.

"It may seem funny to you," he said, grinning sheepishly. "But it hurt like hell."

Reluctantly, he showed us his wound. It had begun to heal, but you could still see it was a nasty bite. No wonder he made all that racket when he jumped off. It was a wonder he hadn't landed in the ocean.

10

~~~~~~

Although we were now well over two-thirds of the way to
Australia, our troubles were just beginning. Most of the dangerous reefs and banks were still ahead of us; so were the
heavy storms. Here we would have to steer our way ever-so-
cautiously past ten major reef barriers, no fewer than nine of
them by night, when our navigation could not afford to be
wrong. According to our maps, some of the jagged reefs were
only five feet out of the water but as much as twenty miles
long, menacing irregular-shaped masses of coral that resembled immense petrified amoebas.

If my daily readings of latitude and longitude, stu-
diously compared with those on my navigation charts, were
faulty by four or five minutes of arc (one minute of arc is
equal to one maritime mile—1,852 meters), the first we

would know about a reef might be a terrible crash in the dark. Small wonder that we would later think of our voyage as *un viaje de noche,* journey by night!

We had wanted to come down in latitude after leaving Savaii, but a stiff south wind on the afternoon of September 15 kept us going northwest. Blowing stronger and stronger as day wore on, creating waves twenty feet high, the wind threatened to push us toward Pasco Bank, less than sixty miles ahead.

"That's a dangerous bank," I told Gabriel, pointing it out on my map. "The sea there is only forty feet deep in spots, and in bad weather the waves drag all the water in and then suddenly slam it down again."

"Could the raft take it?" he asked.

"I'm not sure," I answered, knowing full well it could be smashed to bits. "And I'm not anxious to find out."

But suddenly we had more immediate worries than Pasco Bank. On our radio (still receiving but not transmitting) we got a report from a New Zealand meteorologist predicting winds of forty-five to fifty miles an hour—"a very intense high pressure belt running east to west near the Fiji Islands."

Yelling "batten down the hatches," I hurriedly sealed the radio in eight plastic bags and secured it to the ceiling of the cabin, while Gabriel pulled in the sail and Marc and Normand secured various other items with rope and plastic in accordance with prior arrangements. We worked quietly and efficiently, knowing that time was of the essence. Twenty minutes later we were as ready as possible, though painfully aware that one can never be entirely prepared for the kinds of storms one encounters in the South Pacific— particularly on a raft.

There was an ominous lull in the weather that lasted through dinner, which we ate distractedly and mechanically, conversing in monosyllables with anxious eyes on the dark horizon. Then just before sunset, heavy clouds gathered, and a long moaning wind came out of the east, straight and steady at first, gradually building in volume. As the velocity increased in multiples, it started to twist and screech like a *llorona*. The mere sound chilled me to the bone, reminding me of the *lloronas* I'd been told about as a child, demented witches lost in the night, running through narrow black alleys with blood-curdling screams of inutterable loneliness.

"Parece una bruja," whispered Gabriel, obviously thinking of the witches in his own childhood. "I've never heard such strange winds."

They were now blowing at full gale force of forty to fifty miles per hour, pushing waves more than thirty feet high and whirling *La Balsa* around like a matchbox. Thundering toward us at thirty or forty miles per hour, the waves would build to giant crests of thrashing foam, then come rumbling down with a roaring, ear-shattering noise such as I'd never heard before. There was power enough in each wave to light a small city for an hour. Unless one has been caught in bad seas on a small raft, it's probably impossible to imagine what it's like. Certainly none of us had ever had such an experience.

Thinking it might be safer than staying outside, we crawled into our fragile cabin and waited for the onslaught that was sure to come. All we could see through the doorway was the gush and foam of waves slashing at us from all directions, twisting and turning the raft with a slapping up-and-down motion that bounced us around inside the cabin like loose dice. The floor would tilt forty-five degrees, first sliding us into a helpless heap against one wall, then slamming us against the opposite wall as huge masses of water poured through the doorway and out the windows, drenching us again and again. It would let up for a moment and then blast us again.

At one point an enormous wave hurtled through the portside window and smashed Marc's head against the radio. His mouth opened in a soundless scream, then he sank to his knees and crumpled to the floor as if dead.

"Marc!" I yelled, reaching for him in a sudden rush of fear.

Then to my great relief, I realized he was still breathing, that he'd only been knocked unconscious. But it took me five or six minutes to revive him, holding him against my shoulder to cushion him against the constant onrush of waves crashing into the cabin. Finally he came out of it, groggily shaking his head like a punch-drunk boxer, mumbling "Where am I?"

"On *La Balsa*," I said. "You're still here, Marc. You were knocked out by a wave."

He pondered my answer for a moment, closing his eyes as if to concentrate, then suddenly opened them in full consciousness.

He rose to his knees, then sat back on his haunches again, feeling wobbly as the raft lurched back and forth. Leaning against a side wall, he gripped a corner beam for support as the raft continued to lurch and pivot wildly. The deafening noise of wind and waves made conversation impossible, but to my shouted "All right?" he nodded a vigorous affirmative.

By some miracle our bamboo cabin held fast, creaking and groaning like a dying man, bending and unbending with each fierce gust of wind, straining at the ropes that held it together. No modern cabin would have withstood such pressure—nor even a conventional metal structure. They would have no "give," no capacity to shift with the winds.

But, while the gale raged around us, we had no way of knowing how long or how well the cabin would hold up. We could only pray and hope—and curse. And that's exactly what I did. Yelling into a momentary silence, as the storm refueled itself for another assault, I shook my fist at the ceiling and challenged the gods:

"Come down here, damn it! Come down, and see what it's like!"

But the only response I got was the shrill fury of new winds and the rumble of giant waves making a strange whirring sound. Leaning toward the water-sprayed doorway, Minet perked his ears as if to ascertain the source of this new sound.

"That's the bigger waves curling in on themselves," said Marc. "The big ones don't break—they curl inside like a wheel, with a great whirring noise."

The storm pounded us for hours, giving us a respite now and then, but coming back again and again with awesome force. We sat it out in almost total darkness, confined to the ever-flooding cabin like marooned prisoners, realizing we might be capsized at any moment.

"I never dreamed it would be like this," said Gabriel. No regret in his voice—just a simple matter-of-fact statement.

"Neither did I, Gabriel," I said—for how could anyone imagine such fury?

Eventually, an hour or so before sunrise, the storm subsided to a mild uproar. The waves had shrunk from forty to fifty feet to a mere six or seven feet, and we were able to leave the cabin for a quick survey of the damage.

"The boom has split again," said Marc, running his hand over a previous crack that he had bound with heavy rope. "But it's not a new crack, thank God."

Two supply boxes were splintered, the bamboo deck mat badly shredded, banana leaves ripped off the cabin roof, minor debris everywhere, and scores of wall-eyed sardines flapping between exposed logs. Inside the cabin were several more sardines, a dead flying fish, books with wet and torn pages, and water-soaked sleeping bags that smelled worse than ever.

"Time for spring house cleaning," said Gabriel.

"It's mid-September," I reminded him.

"I know that," he answered. "But this is the southern hemisphere. And it's springtime here."

Occupied with such trivia, we found it easier to ignore the danger that was still with us in the ominous rush of gray clouds coming from the east. So we house cleaned our raft as it roller-coasted from one wave to another, keeping a wary eye on the horizon. Marc moved more slowly than usual, his footsteps still a bit unsteady. Obviously, he had not totally recovered from the injury to his head, and I was reminded of Dr. Fink's warning about brain concussions.

"Take it easy," I told him offhandedly. "Go take a wet nap in my water bag."

"We all need a nap," he said, sighing deeply and rubbing his moist beard. "Nobody slept last night."

Nor did we sleep the following night.

After a long day of minimal winds and quieter waves, during which we lounged on deck trying to keep our minds on a game of Parcheesi, we felt the onset of stiffer winds as the sun was setting on a gray horizon. Once again we huddled inside the cabin, each of us wrapping a rope around his waist and tying it to one of the corner beams.

"I'm not sure how safe this is," I said to Normand. "We might get tangled in the rope when we need to be free—but at least it feels safer."

The second gale struck us a few hours after sundown. Once again the waves swelled to heights of up to fifty feet, washing over us with thunderous force and lifting the raft at precarious angles when they curled under. With water rushing through our cabin, we tried to joke our way through the night, often swallowing great mouthfuls of the punch lines because of the rumbling, whistling noises all around us. Yet we laughed—at times maniacally—the way people laugh when they're dead tired or terribly frightened, though I can honestly say that I had gone beyond that point of fear. I felt the danger, yes, but no fear. There was, instead, a conviction that we would pass this awful test, that our journey would be meaningless without it, that perhaps St. Francis himself had sent these winds as a kind of baptismal ritual.

"Chisco," I said half aloud. "You're a true rascal."

"Are you talking to that saint again?" asked Gabriel.

"Thanking him," I answered, "for this fine storm."

He told me later that he was sure the winds had driven me crazy.

In our preoccupation with the storm, nobody noticed that Minet had suddenly disappeared. It was Marc who first noticed his absence.

"I haven't heard Minet lately," he said. "Is he frightened?"

"Normand has him," said Gabriel, unable to see in the darkness.

"No, *you* have him," said Normand.

Gabriel jumped up and lunged past me, calling "Minet! Minet!" as he staggered through an incoming mass of water at the doorway.

"Pull him back, Vital," hollered Marc. "He'll be washed overboard!"

Yanking with all my strength I managed to get Gabriel back with Normand's help. "Minet will be all right," said Marc with as much conviction as possible. "He's a tough cat."

But Gabriel wouldn't be consoled.

"He's drowned," he said, making his way back to his corner.

He said nothing more the rest of the night, but we knew he was miserable. I also felt sad, and for all the deafening noises outside, there was an empty silence inside the cabin.

The gale was gone before dawn, and an eerie calm greeted us when we crawled outside at daybreak. The sky was still gray, but the waves were down to an acceptable choppiness. As I stood there, accustoming myself to the sudden quiet, I heard a tentative anxious "meow."

Looking up, I saw Minet clinging to one of the slanting mast posts, his limbs wrapped around it like a baby bear on a tree.

"Minet! Minet!" yelled Gabriel. "Come down."

Perhaps too frightened or exhausted to move, Minet wouldn't budge; and finally Gabriel shinnied up the pole and brought him down, tears welling in his eyes. Forgetting our fatigue, we cheered and laughed and caressed our tenacious little mascot. We would never know how long he had been on the mast, whether he had climbed up after hiding

Vital takes a noon navigational sight.

Marc makes an entry in the log. Note the balsa "head."

Vital and Gabriel cut fillets from a juicy dorado.

Vital, Gabriel, and Marc around the Parcheesi board.

Gabriel and Vital stow fruit given them by Samoans.

The crew trims ship to catch a new breeze from astern.

Marc secures rigging in preparation for a tropical squall.

Minet is introduced to a
denizen of the sea.

works a *guara* to
ge course through
h seas.

Vital and Normand man rear *guaras*.

Vital and friend inspect catch for midday meal.

A relaxing moment

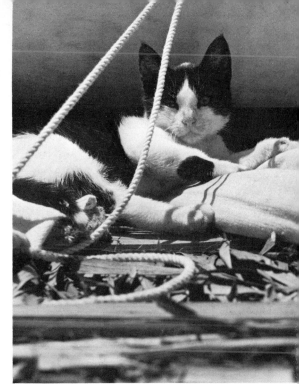

A swelling sea brings
warning of advancing
storm.

LATE
FINAL
EXTRA

THE SUN

TURN TO PAGE

Telephone 2 0944, Jones Street, Broadway, Letters to Box 506, GPO, Sydney, 2001.

CITY FORECAST: Warm.   ● Lottery: Special No. 1958, page 78   ● Finance, page 40   ● TV, pa

8,564 MILES ON THIS!

BIG HOPE FOR THE SUBURBS

CASH FOR JET NOISE

WHETHER people plagued by aircraft get money to shut out the noise depends on a new move today. The Premier, Mr Askin, has asked the Commonwealth for special financial aid. Continued page 2.

There were gasps of astonishment from spectators when La Balsa was pulled from the water for the last time on the Brisbane River yesterday. Bystanders were amazed that such a frail craft could have drifted 8,564 miles.

A huge shark smashed a crewman through the wall of La Balsa's cabin in a fierce Pacific storm.

The shark — one of a pack which had circled La Balsa for weeks — reared from the water on a wave and lunged at the man working on the raft.

The man was dashed to the log floor, bleeding and half conscious.

The shark followed the swell back into the water.

This incident — one of a thousand chilling moments — will be retold exactly as it happened in the Captain's account of La Balsa's great voyage beginning in Sunday's "Sun-Herald."

THE LOG
LA BA

THE LOG OF
BALSA will be
issued in "The Su
next week.

On Monday
will be four o
pages of absorbing
pictures taken b
crew. Cost p 2.

An Australian newspaper hails completion of *La Balsa*'s voyage.

somewhere or whether he had spent that awful night clinging to the pole for dear life. Suffice it to say, he had proved
himself an awfully tough *hombre*.

The storm retreated for several hours; but it came back
at mid-afternoon, not as violent as before but strong enough
to cause more trouble. My navigation log for the seventeenth
of September reports that Marc was tossed overboard shortly
after he assumed his regular watch at 6:00 P.M. He had been
extremely nervous and tired, and his fingers were swollen
and blistered from tightening the knots on our cabin. Consequently, when the raft lurched abruptly he had lost his grip
on the starboard *guara* and tumbled backwards off the stern,
yelling *"a l'aide!"*

Scrambling across the slippery deck, Normand and I
quickly pulled him in by the rope around his waist, straining every muscle in our weary arms.

"Merci, mes amis!" he said laughingly when he was
safely aboard. "That was a poor time to take a bath."

"Especially without soap," I said. "But we forgive you
this time."

But we wouldn't have been able to forgive ourselves if
he had drowned, for we should have insisted (rather than
merely urged) that he let one of us take over his watch. He
was much too tired, and probably not fully recovered from
his concussion.

"Marc," I said, determined to correct that omission. "As
captain of this ship, I must order you to quarters. We can't afford a tired chief cook. You're liable to poison us."

Obviously aware of the real intent behind my attempt
at humor, he smiled and crawled into the cabin for whatever
rest was possible on that miserable choppy sea. My reference
to his cooking was rather ironic under the circumstances, for

161

none of us did any cooking during those three days of stormy weather. We subsisted on what remained of the fresh fruit and native bread we had gotten at Savaii, rationing it in meager daily portions that failed to curb our hunger. How we yearned for fried, or even raw, fish.

Aside from the hunger, we all felt an enormous weariness, a soreness in every muscle of our bodies, and, like Marc, our hands were swollen and cut from tightening all the connecting ropes and from continually hoisting and lowering the sail. The cordage, as one might expect in such volatile weather, would be slack one minute and then tight enough to snap a few minutes later. One could hear a symphony of different sounds as the escalating winds twanged on the taut ropes. When the thin ropes vibrated in high pitch, you knew the wind was strong. When the half-inch ropes *thummmed,* the wind was very strong; and when you heard the inch-and-a-half ropes *thonggg,* it was time to batten the hatches. Since an inch-and-a-half nylon rope can sustain a weight of 4,800 pounds, the wind would have to be fierce to make it *thooonggg* like a giant bass-viol cord.

We finally got a spell of good weather on the eighteenth of September, enabling me to get a fix on our longitude and latitude.

"I hope we haven't strayed too far," I said, my eyes trained on the tiny numbers on my sextant. "We might be headed for Japan."

The storm, I soon discovered, had been pushing us northwest toward an area clotted with banks, but we had apparently skirted Pasco Bank on the night of September 15. Now we were safely bypassing Isabella Bank, another treacherous reef. It was strange to see Spanish names way out here in the middle of the South Pacific. We Spaniards dropped names everywhere.

My log reflects our change in mood:

September 19:
The sun comes out. We have blue skies and a blue sea. We are happy again (although Minet is sick and has lost some weight). We have won another battle with the sea, and we laugh. But every day we have more respect for this immense natural force.
The wind has changed just in time. It has been pushing us northwest, but now it has shifted to the east and we begin to come down a bit in latitude.

We wanted to come down as close as we could to the northern coasts of Vanua Levu and Viti Levu, two of the principal Fiji Islands, then go vertically so as to pass south of New Caledonia. There would be fewer islands and reefs that way, and we would miss Australia's famous Great Barrier Reef.

We had now been some fifteen weeks on the high seas, and we had acquired a new kind of courage, the cool tested-by-fire courage of a seasoned *matador* as opposed to the defiant courage of a young *novillero,* who is still trying to convince himself that he's not afraid of bulls. Like good *matadores,* we were adjusting our styles to the individual quirks of each new storm, trying to maintain that "grace under pressure" which Ernest Hemingway described so well. For him—as for us—false bravado was merely the other face of panic.

Marc responded to my hispanic analogy with typical gallic skepticism. "But you've got to remember," he said. "That

163

even Manolete finally met a Miura." (Manolete was killed in Linares in 1947 by a bull from the Miura ranch, which reputedly raised the most dangerous bulls in Spain.)

"Then we shall die like Manolete," I said. "And with grace, I hope."

Recalling the faraway Sunday afternoon in my childhood when I saw Manolete thrilling the *aficionados* of Santander while I watched with bated breath, tugging my father's sleeve, I started humming a bullfight song as I scrubbed the residue of seaweed from the logs near the bow. Because of a continuing accumulation of seaweed and other foliage, the deck had become as slippery as a wall-to-wall carpet of banana peels. Nourished by a constant supply of plankton and algae, the various kinds of plant life under the raft had crept through crevices between the logs to form another miniature jungle aboveboard. On calm days we could scrape away most of the new growth, but the recent storms had made scraping impossible. Consequently, we had more than enough work to keep us busy. But no matter how hard we scraped, the logs became more and more slippery as our journey progressed. We moved about with flat-footed caution, legs wide apart and arms held out to cushion a possible fall.

Naturally, we all had moments of carelessness, when we would forget to brace ourselves, and Normand had such a moment a few days after the gale. He was standing near the bow watching Minet tease a sardine, and was kneeling for a closer look when a wave jolted the raft, causing him to slip sideways into the water.

"Man overboard!" I shouted, scrambling and slipping as I rushed forward.

But he was nowhere to be seen when I finally reached

the bow. Marc and Gabriel quickly joined me, and all three of us nervously scanned the choppy sea in search of Normand, afraid to express the horror we felt, each one inwardly convinced a shark had probably grabbed him, that he was dying a horrible death somewhere under the raft.

"I'll dive in," said Marc.

"No—I will," I said, reaching for a rope to tie around my waist. "You're still sick."

"I'll go," said Gabriel, reaching for another rope.

But our brief debate was unnecessary. With a shout of triumph, Normand crawled onto the stern behind us. *"Voilà! Le champion de la mer!"*

He had allowed the current to take him under the raft from bow to stern, accumulating a fantastic wig of seaweed and plankton along the way. It had been a mere frolic for him. The possibility of sharks had never entered his mind.

As my log indicates, the next few days were free of actual danger, but we seemed to be headed for serious trouble.

September 23:

We have come down a few degrees in latitude, but not enough. A rather stiff current pushes us west. The navigation chart indicates this current goes south at half a knot, but for us it is going west at two and a half knots. I don't like it.

September 28:

The wind is good, but it's a pity we have gone so far north of Viti Levu. We dream of passing south of New Caledonia. If we can't do that, we will have great problems because of the corals and reefs.

As every sailor knows, the New Hebrides, northeast of New Caledonia, are a chain of volcanic islands some four hundred miles long, a nightmare for even those vessels with sophisticated instruments. I had no desire to try to navigate them in a raft.

September 30:

We are coming down nicely. The wind is from the east, accompanied by a slight current. I ask Normand what he thinks of the wind and he says, "Oh boooooy!" But thoughts of New Caledonia—the need to get south of it—occupy our minds and conversation. Thinking about this problem, I sleep only one or two hours each night.

October 1:

To clear the southern tip of New Caledonia we will need a course of 200 degrees, and to do this we need a wind from the east or northeast—*not the south wind that blows today!*

"We cry against the Devil, against God and against nature! And where is Chisco now that we need him?"

~~~~~~~~

11

While I fretted about contrary winds that might prevent us from skirting the southern fringe of the New Caledonia area, Marc had a more immediate personal worry. His supply of cigarettes and tobacco had been drenched by salt water during the storm, and again he was edgy and short-tempered, having had nothing to smoke for thirty-six hours. On the first sunny day after the storm he carefully slit open the damaged cigarettes and spread the wet tobacco on a flat pan, which he anchored to the cabin roof so it would have maximum exposure to the hot sun.

"I'm glad you brought along your hippie cigarette paper," he said to Gabriel, who had been rolling his own before giving up smoking for Marc's benefit.

"I hope it's still dry," said Gabriel.

"Don't worry about that," Marc said. "I keep the packet inside the camera bags." (He was referring to the eight plastic bags which encased our camera and film.)

By mid-afternoon the tobacco was dry enough for three dozen cigarettes, which Marc rolled with great skill and speed, hungrily chain-smoking the first four while he made the rest. Then he relaxed a bit and started to pace his smoking for the long run.

Gabriel was busy again with his diary and a few poems, softly humming to himself as he sat back to ponder a new phrase. Meanwhile, Normand had spent several hours trying to catch a large swordfish which had been trailing us since daybreak, racing past us to starboard with its two sharp-pointed fins jutting from the water five feet apart, then gracefully pivoting to come straight up with menacing speed. A few feet away it would dive and swoop under *La Balsa,* occasionally grazing one of the centerboards before emerging ten or fifteen feet beyond the stern. Again and again, it repeated the pattern, its seven-foot sword piercing the water with deadly precision, though every now and then it would churn and thrash about like a playful dolphin.

"I've been trying to hook him," Normand told me. "But he won't take my bait."

"He's not hungry enough," I said. "Though he soon will be, with all that thrashing around."

Eventually, the swordfish swept closer to us and snagged Normand's bait without touching the hook itself. But as it turned away from us, a huge gray shark torpedoed out of the depths and chomped off the swordfish's tail in one fierce bite. Mortally wounded without its propelling agent, the swordfish was soon devoured in a bloody turmoil just below the surface.

"There goes our dinner," said Normand glumly.

"How about some shark meat?" suggested Marc. "Plenty of nice filets out there."

"Not today. That killer's too big and mean. I couldn't handle him."

Normand was probably right: our lack of sleep and nourishment during the three-day storm had weakened us. The sharks we had caught were generally six to ten feet long, some of them blue-gray and others a dirty brown. Tough-skinned and muscular, they were difficult to slice, and we always tried for their most vulnerable spot—the five gill clefts behind the head on both sides. Some of them were covered with scores of remora fish, black slippery parasites who would fasten themselves to the larger fish by means of a vacuum disc on top of their flat heads. Their hold was so tight it was difficult to scrape them off, but they themselves would eventually break away and wriggle between the logs back to the sea. Once in a while we found remora fish vacuum-stuck to one of our logs, apparently mistaking it for a fish.

Strangely enough, Minet showed no interest in them; perhaps he was repulsed by their parasitic nature. But his never-ending fascination with crabs finally got him in trouble. One afternoon Normand managed to catch a large crab, which immediately attracted Minet's attention. Betrayed by a faulty sense of proportion he started batting at it, when suddenly the crab snared his left forepaw with one of its large claws, and Minet let out a series of loud meows as he scrambled around the deck, slapping his free paw in a vain attempt to break the viselike grip. Finally, Normand rescued him by chopping off the crab's claw and prying it loose.

"Minet," he said, "you're a damned fool."

Apparently chagrined, Minet crept away and avoided us the rest of the afternoon. In fact, he disappeared from sight altogether, and all we could hear was an occasional faint meow coming from somewhere behind the cabin.

"He's punishing us," said Marc. "He's hiding, hoping we'll think he's gone or dead."

He continued to "punish" us for several hours but the meows got louder and more impatient as the sun began to set. Then, with a look of cool disdain, he surfaced from his hiding place and strutted up and down the deck.

"Don't laugh," I said with a straight face. "Or he'll go into hiding again."

We wouldn't have had time for an encore of Minet's act; another storm was brewing on the horizon. Dark clouds gathered swiftly and soon broke out in heavy rain, whipped across the deck by gusts of wind from the north. We barely had time to haul in the sail before the stronger winds came, rattling the loose boom against the mast. Gabriel and I stayed on deck, holding the steering oar between us, while Marc and Normand tried to rest for the second night watch.

"Doesn't look too bad," said Gabriel, no doubt comparing it with the previous storm. "I'll bet these winds are less than twenty miles an hour."

"Strong enough," I said, binding a rope around my waist and fastening it to the nearest crossbeam.

We bounced around for several hours in the darkness, listening to the keening twang of the guy ropes as the winds grew stronger, bracing our legs for the onslaught of waves cascading over us in blinding foam. Beneath our callus-hardened feet we could feel the logs jostling up and down like piano keys, rhythmically accommodating the rumbling seas. We could also hear the creaks and groans of our bamboo cabin, valiantly resisting the multiple stresses of wind and waves.

"I like it better outside," said Gabriel. "You feel so helpless inside the cabin."

I had to agree. Outside you could at least meet the danger head-on; you had the illusion of possible self-defense. But we couldn't have stayed on deck during a full gale; we would have been tossed overboard every five minutes. In a squall like this, however, it was relatively safe.

"Let's keep the watch all night," suggested Gabriel. "They both need a rest—especially Marc."

"Good idea," I said, noting that the squall was already subsiding. "It should be fairly easy from now on."

Shortly after daybreak Marc and Normand crawled out of the cabin to relieve us.

"Why didn't you call us?" mumbled Marc, his eyes squinting at the sun.

"We forgot," I said. "Gabriel was telling me about the beautiful women in Santiago and Valparaiso, and we forgot all about the time."

He scolded us, but we happily accepted his fatherly grumpiness. "We're going to have a great dinner tonight," Gabriel predicted before falling off into deep slumber. "Grandpa looks like a new man."

When we arose at mid-afternoon, refreshed and hungry, Marc told us he was feeling much better but that the raft was in failing health. "The logs seem looser, Vital. All these storms have stretched the ropes and cut the grooves deeper."

We checked ten or twelve grooves on the starboard and portside logs and found that the ropes had indeed carved much deeper into the balsa wood, accounting for a certain looseness between the seven main logs. Though it was too early to know for sure, the deeper cuts could conceivably absorb water because they hadn't been sealed with oil.

While the logs still had lost very little floatability, the looseness of the crossbeams and bottom logs, plus the deeper rope grooves, were cause for considerable worry as we headed on our zigzag course through the dangerous reefs ahead. A tight firm raft would have been far easier to maneuver.

On October 5, we realized that we wouldn't be able to pass south of New Caledonia. Thus knowing we had to plan our course three hundred to four hundred miles ahead, I decided to steer between the islands of Eromanga and Tana in the southern New Hebrides, and then shift north of the Loyalty Islands.

"That passage will be narrow and dangerous," I explained to Gabriel, who had been studying the maps with me. "There are all kinds of uncharted reefs there. But perhaps some French music will help us to relax." Although our radio transmitter was still dead, the receiver worked fairly well, allowing us to hear occasional broadcasts from Noumea, the capital of New Caledonia.

With our sail set at a northwesterly slant and the centerboards positioned for a similar direction, we stood at the prow of our little raft as it bounced and dipped toward the lowering sun, searching for some sign of the two islands we had to pass between.

"If we could see them before dark, it would be easier," said Gabriel, absentmindedly stroking Minet.

"But I'm afraid we won't," said Marc. "The sun is going down fast."

The sunset was beautiful that afternoon, fluffy flame-tinted clouds escorting a bright orange disc beyond the horizon. I could have sworn the earth was flat, that the sun was falling off the edge into endless space. But when it was gone, we had not seen a trace of Eromanga or Tana and the wind was beginning to shift.

"Damn it, Chisco," I muttered half aloud. "We'll be sailing blind. Why must we always face these dangers at night?"

None of us could sleep—we all stood watch—and there was no music from Noumea to relieve the tension. Marc and I stood at the corners of the bow, peering into the darkness for either of the two islands and periodically stooping down to look for the tell-tale splash of waves against hidden reefs. Normand and Gabriel were stationed at the stern, alternating turns at the starboard *guara,* prepared to shift course if necessary. Near midnight I thought I saw a splash against a dark reef, but it was only a shark's dorsal fin cutting a foamy circle around the raft. He was soon joined by another, and they trailed us for hours, like vultures hovering around a prospective corpse. Tightening the life rope around my waist, I concentrated once again on the dark horizon, vainly searching for the invisible contours of the islands.

"Eromanga and Tana," mused Marc. "Are you sure they exist?"

"They do on my map," I said, although I had to admit they sounded a bit like something out of *Alice in Wonderland*.

But an hour later, just after daybreak, Gabriel verified the existence of Eromanga. Pointing to the tip of an island on the horizon behind us and slightly northeast, he said, "Look, we passed it last night."

The island of Tana, behind us to the southeast, was not even visible.

Now we had to get by the famous Astrolabe Reefs, which lay midway between Tana and the even-more-dangerous Petrie Reef.

We skirted the northern frings of the Astrolabe Reefs on the late afternoon of the following day, coming close enough to see the jagged coral blocks jutting from the frothy waves for several miles. At one particular spot, where the reef stretched toward us like an accusing finger, I studied the strange formations through my powerful binoculars. It looked like an immense rock garden pitted with anemones and coral, with tufts of fossilized plants in various hues of purple, yellow, green, and red; dark green mosses here and there, and prickly objects that resembled cactus. With the lens at full magnification, I saw thousands of brilliant sea shells, pink corals, sea slugs, and small sharks chasing fish of all sizes, shapes, and colors—a fantasy of strange flora and fauna that only the sea can provide.

Turning northwest, we headed for the treacherous passage between Petrie Reef and the French Reefs, about two and a half days away. We naturally hoped to make it by daylight, but my navigational calculations indicated another night of tension and uncertainty.

True to expectations, we drew near Petrie Reef after sundown, unable to see it but hoping we were at least three or four miles south of it. A strong steady wind from the southeast increased our speed, but it also created choppy waves that gave us a jerky seesaw motion. Once again we all shared the night watch, but with the darkness and the six-foot waves, we couldn't have sighted a reef a hundred yards away.

Fortunately, we held to a fairly steady course, and at dawn we saw the jagged silhouette of the reef behind us, although its position indicated we had passed dangerously close. The wind was coming from the east, but the current was running strongly northwest, making it impossible for us to get through Grand Passage, directly west of Petrie Reef.

"We'll have to go northwest of the D'Entrecasteaux Reefs and Huon Island," I told Gabriel. "That ought to test the raft. It's one of the trickiest seas in the world."

We contacted Rafael Corcuera in Mexico by radio on the evening of October 10. Using our time-consuming click-click system, we told him our approximate position, not knowing we were less than nine miles from the dreaded D'Entrecasteaux Reefs. Then, as we were signing off, I heard the voice of a New Zealand ham operator named Gus. He was talking to Rafael, but we could hear him quite clearly.

"They're in danger!" he said. "They're headed straight for the reef—less than nine miles away!"

Then Samuel Fernandez's voice broke in. "New Zealand, New Zealand, I agree with you . . . they are in great danger . . . The wind is from the east and pushing them hard toward the reef . . . We've got to warn them . . . Their radio is out . . . Can you call Noumea to send a plane?"

It was already quite dark when we heard the urgent plea from Mexico City. Once again we were headed for a possible disaster in the moonless night, to spend another sleepless ten hours standing watch at the corners of the raft. The seas were relatively calm, the wind was cool and steady. Once in a while, when the moon would break through a rift in the clouds, we could see a huge shark trailing a few feet behind the stern, no doubt attracted by the remainder of the dolphin we had eaten for dinner. Marc was saving a portion for tomorrow's lunch.

"He looks mean and hungry," said Gabriel. "I hope he's around in the morning. I'll catch him myself."

But the shark was gone before daybreak. And the reefs of D'Entrecasteaux were far behind us, barely visible through our binoculars. But around 11 A.M. we could hear a small plane somewhere in the vicinity of the reefs. Five hours later, when we again made a one-way contact with our ham-radio network, I heard a voice saying, "The plane didn't find anything. So I think they made it okay. If they had hit the reef, there would have been some wreckage."

I tried to reassure them, but they were apparently unable to hear the clicking from our not-too-reliable transmitter. After a half hour of futile tampering with the salt-encrusted coils, I went back to my navigation charts to ascertain our next move. We were now headed for the Huon Islands, and I calculated we would probably reach them late in the afternoon. My log offers a different picture:

October 12:

We have passed the Huon Islands and their reefs—again during the night. Incredible! I think somebody is pushing us. I can no longer sleep at night. I'm afraid to be awakened by the crunching of the raft against a reef.

The wind is from the east, but we cannot go south as far as we would like because the current is flowing due west. We would like to go almost due south so as to miss Chesterfield Reef and Islets, which are between five and seventeen feet high.

Passing a reef at night you must know your position exactly. Your chronometer must be perfect because one second's difference means an error of a quarter of a mile. Eight seconds is two miles. (We were using Greenwich Mean

Time, which we got from our radio.) At night you must be within half a mile to see the surf breaking on a reef, and then it is likely to be too late to change course on a raft such as ours with no motor.

With each new test, however, we became prouder of our raft's performance. Its nine centerboards were working better than ever. We found the starboard stern centerboard the most useful one for correcting deviation to the left, and the next most important was the portside stern *guara*. But all the *guaras* were extremely useful, and, in certain conditions of wind and current, indispensable.

October 13:

No wind today. We can rest, and let the small current take us south from Huon Island. We sang songs all afternoon, ate a fine lunch of flying fish prepared by Marc, played Parcheesi for high stakes.

Gabriel says, "We are lucky for once."

And Marc says, "If we are lucky now, I am afraid what will happen tomorrow."

Marc was right, but it would be a different kind of trouble than he expected.

12

~~~~~~~~

On the following day we drifted into a dead sea again. There was no current and no breeze. I lit a match and the flame was perfectly vertical. The sun, suspended high above us in a cloudless sky, was unbearably hot, forcing us to seek the meager shade provided by the shadow of the cabin. Nothing seemed to be moving in that torpid heat except a few cockroaches and ants, which even Minet was too listless to bother, preferring to nap in the slowly-shifting shadow of the mast.

Glancing at a cockroach near his bare feet, Gabriel was reminded of a dreary desert in Chile. "It's called Antofagasta, the dryest place in the world. Only cockroaches can survive there. They crack under your shoes like peanut shells."

So saying, he half raised his heel as if to smash the intruder, but seemingly lacked the energy to do so.

"This damned sun will kill us," he said. "I'm getting red spots in front of my eyes."

"Why don't you go inside the cabin?"

"It's like a furnace."

So we stayed in the sun, shifting now and then when the cockroaches or ants pestered us too much, but otherwise lying as still as the dead gray water around us. There were no fish anywhere; they had disappeared along with the current. Thus deprived of our daily catch, we had fish from the day before, eating it raw so as not to produce any additional heat from the stove. It was warm and bitter. Neither Marc nor I could eat it, but Normand and Gabriel cleaned their plates as if it were their last meal, chewing the tough pieces with a stubborn, joyless determination. I knew of Gabriel's phobia about starving, and I now suspected that Normand shared the same fear.

Sunset brought some relief from the scorching heat, but there was still no breeze to ease our torpor. Nor was there wind or current the following morning. My sextant indicated that we had moved less than a mile in twenty-four hours.

"Why don't we row?" asked Gabriel. "This will drive us crazy."

"Be patient," Marc said. "We're bound to get a breeze before the day is over. We can't afford to waste the little energy we've got left.

But even Marc grew a bit apprehensive as the sun got hotter and the air remained windless. The sea was like a stagnant pond, with scarcely a ripple to signify life. Finally, just after the burning sun slipped over the horizon, we got a cooling breeze from the north. Not enough to billow the sail but enough to allay our fears. Two hours later we drifted into a southerly current, and the wind increased enough to push us along at a comfortable five-mile pace. We sang "La Cucaracha" and "La Marseillaise," our voices tumbling over each other like carefree waves.

The next few days were almost perfect. The sun was bright but not too hot, the wind from the northeast strong and steady, the fish plentiful, and the current favorable for the course we had charted. We were headed for a passage north of the Chesterfield Reefs, confident that *La Balsa* could navigate the narrowest spaces and the roughest seas.

"We're less than seven hundred miles from Australia," I told Marc after checking our position on my sextant. "And the raft is still in fine shape."

"A bit loose here and there though," he reminded me, tapping the mast with his knuckles. "Also needs a shave."

The ragged beards of seaweed had grown up again on the outside logs, shaggy green tufts that trailed in the water collecting plankton, barnacles, and algae. We had abandoned our daily scraping chore, lazily allowing nature to take its course.

"We ought to take some pictures before it gets a haircut," said Gabriel.

A half hour later, having carefully removed the camera from its plastic covers, Gabriel and I hopped into the dinghy and rowed several hundred yards away from the bow. From that distance it looked terribly fragile and primitive, hardly seaworthy enough to cross the English Channel, much less an ocean. Picturing the four of us huddled inside that bamboo cabin like blind mules, being bounced and buffeted by forty-foot waves, I realized we had lost all perspective. We couldn't possibly have known the true size and nature of the danger around us, or the meagerness of our protection. But of course *La Balsa* was all we had—our whole world. One always exaggerates the size of his world. "I've been thinking about that gale," mused Gabriel as if he were privy to my thoughts. "It was really worse than I imagined."

"How so?" I asked.

"I don't know how to say it exactly. It's just a funny feeling I got a minute ago, a strange sort of chill when I looked at the raft. Silly I guess."

"Maybe not," I said. "Tell me about it."

"Well, it looks so small from here—like a toy. And when you think of those huge waves and the wind blowing like it could knock down a house. You wonder why we didn't get killed. I mean it doesn't make any sense."

"Did you think we'd be killed?"

"I don't think so. I was too scared to think about dying."

"You didn't seem scared."

He paused, fiddled with the roll of film. "But that's what I felt just now. That cold feeling."

"We all get that," I said, taking the film from him and inserting it into the camera. "Some people call it shell shock. It's like a soldier convincing himself he's not scared when the bombs are exploding all around him. He sucks in the fear and keeps on fighting—but the fear comes back later on."

We closed the subject and started snapping pictures of the raft, Gabriel rowing while I worked the camera, and vice versa. There was a certain comic elegance about *La Balsa* as we came closer, a sort of quixotic flair in the billowing sail that contrasted with the shabbiness of the cabin. Dali's painting, glittering in its plastic casing, was a bold challenge to all evil, and I felt that the legendary Man from La Mancha would have been proud to sail on our little raft.

"She's the most beautiful raft in the world," said Gabriel.

I had to agree. It was a good little craft and had held up through remarkably severe conditions. Nevertheless, I couldn't help fretting about the looseness Marc and I had detected. Especially at night. Lying still on the mat inside the cabin with little else to distract me, I could feel a jostling between the logs as if the ropes were wearing away. Even the *guaras* had become slightly wobbly, making it more difficult to steer through narrow passages. A friend of mine, Dr. Gomez Medina, once told me that bodily disintegration generally increases at a geometric progression (1, 2, 4, 8, 16, 32, and so on) rather than a numerical, and I wondered if the same process applied to objects as well. Would the ropes and logs suddenly give way as we were approaching the dangerous Chesterfield Reefs? Or would they wait until we got to the more dangerous Great Barrier Reef? Although I knew it was useless to dwell on problems that were out of our control, the creaks of straining ropes would sometimes keep me awake like distant police sirens in a lonely city.

Why must our worries intensify at night, when we are presumably at peace? Not once did I worry that way during the daylight hours, not even during the worst gales. When the darkness was gone my mind was apt to dwell on more pleasant things, such as curious cloud formations which often resembled familiar profiles or silhouettes of animals. I especially remember certain clouds that looked like fluffy funnels rising from the sea itself, standing still and alone while other clouds drifted by with the trade winds.

"Those are *cumulonimbus* clouds," Marc told Gabriel when he first mentioned them, producing a much-used notebook in which he had scribbled bits of information on various matters related to sailing and marine life. "According to this, they are 'dense, white, fluffy flat-based clouds with multiple rounded tops and well-defined outlines usually formed by the ascent of thermally unstable air masses.'"

Then, noticing the blank look in his eyes, he put aside his notebook and explained that "when the hot tropical sun starts beating down on an island or a fairly large reef, a lot of warm air is created. And after a while it starts to rise— straight up—until its vapor content condenses as it gets to a colder strata of air."

"That's very good, Professor," said Gabriel. "But why does this kind of cloud stand still while all the other clouds are drifting by?"

"Because they're much heavier—even though they have a fluffy look."

"Then we must be near an island," Gabriel said, nodding toward the distant funnel-shaped cloud on the horizon in front of us.

"Not necessarily," Marc replied. "It could be a large reef."

It must be the Chesterfield Reefs," I said, studying my chart and chronometer. I quickly calculated how long it would take us to reach them, and concluded we would have to pass them in the dark.

Once again we stood an all-night vigil, but detected no slashing of waves that might indicate invisible reefs. According to my calculations, however, we must have passed the first of the Chesterfield Reefs around midnight of October 21, and the last just before dawn. We were relieved and further elated when we got a strong morning wind from the east which, combined with a southerly current, would carry us in a southwest direction.

On the night of October 23, we passed Keen Reef, but we somehow changed direction without knowing it. At daybreak we were headed due west instead of southwest, which led me to conclude that we had barely missed a potential disaster on the southern tip of the reef.

The next two days and nights were spent on a zigzag course through lesser reefs. Some, not even charted, were lying just below the surface, like unseen traps—particularly dangerous for minor crafts like ours without radar.

"*La Balsa* has its own radar," observed Marc one afternoon as we twisted through a jagged mass of coral five feet below the surface. "I think she uses the seaweed on her belly as antenna."

Minet (like other sea cats I've heard about) had also developed an internal radar that gave him an amazing ability to predict bad weather many hours before it developed. The sky would be clear, the sun warm and pleasant, but suddenly he would creep into the far corner of the cabin, refusing to join us outside. Several hours later a big squall would come, surprising everyone but Minet. Certain entries in my log testify to this uncanny sense of impending storms.

October 26:

Minet was right again about the weather yesterday. It suddenly rained like hell.

Today we heard for the first time a ham operator in Sidney named Sid Molen. This makes Australia seem much closer. He has a strong voice, and is very brief and practical.

Gabriel was on first night watch, and around midnight he called me loudly: "I see the light of Frederick Reef, Vital. We're about six miles away from it."

We somehow managed to change direction to southwest to avoid crashing into it. The light was a great help. Most reefs have nothing to warn you at night. We all took turns at the sail or with the compass. Half hour on, half hour off. It was pretty tense business. Finally, the sun came up, and we saw the reef behind us. Once again we all started singing "La Marseillaise."

Now we were headed for the Great Barrier Reef, one of the most dangerous areas in the world for any kind of vessel. It was never our intention to approach Australia at this latitude, but it now seemed unavoidable. With Marc peering over my shoulder, I spread our heavily marked navigation chart on the matted deck and carefully studied the jagged profile of the immense reef, searching for a narrow indentation that might indicate a possible passage at high tide. "This light-shaded area might be an opening," I said to Marc with more hope than conviction.

"I doubt it," he responded. "I've been told that there are no safe passages. We'd better prepare for a crash."

"There's still one possibility we haven't considered," I said, pointing to some wavy lines on the chart. "There's a current there that runs south along the eastern face of the reef. We might have a fifteen percent chance of drifting with it."

Marc smiled, baring his tobacco-stained teeth. "How did you reach that precise calculation?"

"Very simple," I answered. "Fifteen is half of thirty—

and thirty per cent is a fair chance. I figure we only have about half a fair chance. Especially if this wind dies down before we get there."

We had been pushed along by a stiff wind from the east, heading directly toward the barrier at six or seven miles per hour. Since we were about seventy-five miles away according to my computations, we would be within sight of the reef an hour before sunset. But if we should pull in the sail to slow down, in order to slide into the coastal current, we would run the risk of a nighttime collision with one of the reef banks that stretched into the current.

"Let's keep the sail up until we actually see the barrier," said Marc. "We'll still have time to slow down. I'd rather face it before dark."

Once again I felt like a matador on the morning of an important *corrida,* wondering how the bulls would behave at four o'clock. Would they be big and powerful, or smaller and more treacherous? One could never know until they charged into the bullring and began searching for the man behind the red *capote.* Perhaps the Great Barrier Reef would be like the Miura bull that killed Manolete—rugged, powerful, mean, and treacherous.

Facing west with my navigation chart unfurled like a *muleta,* I held it forward and then slowly executed a graceful *derechazo* that led an imaginary bull past my waist, as I pivoted for the next pass.

"You Spaniards are all bullfighters," said Gabriel, catching me in mid-act.

"Only in our daydreams. It's safer that way."

Though we stayed under sail, the sky darkened before we could get within sight of the reef, and the wind switched from east to south southeast. Normand had gone up to the crow's nest to scan the horizon with the binoculars, but could see nothing but the amber afterglow of sunset on the choppy waves. Marc and Gabriel were at the boom, trying to swing the sail just enough to change our course without losing the wind. Finally, when it was too dark to see anything more than three hundred feet away, I decided to take in the sail.

"We're liable to hit that reef before we can see it," I said, holding the compass close to my eyes. "We'd better slow down and drift a while. I hope the current is strong enough to save us."

As we got closer to the unseen reef, our sail down and steering oar set for a change in direction, the unwanted winds kept pushing us due west. Having tied down everything in preparation for a crash, we stood at the bow peering into the darkness and praying for a miracle.

"Call your saint, Vital," said Gabriel. "We need him."

There was no jest in his voice. With the fervor of a determined but ambivalent atheist, he was asking me in all seriousness to call upon Saint Francis.

But I made no attempt to communicate with Chisco as we drifted toward the reef. None of us said much of anything. We simply stood near the bow, solemnly staring at the night-shrouded sea, each one lost in his own thoughts. Mine were rather wistful and vague at first. Had we come all this distance—nearly eight thousand miles through the worst obstacles—simply to fail on the last lap? I was reminded of the admonition of the Chinese philosopher Lin Yutang to view life with "a gentle irony." Yet I felt small comfort in his beguiling phrase that night. How could I gently accept the irony of ninety percent success and ten percent failure, when that ten percent canceled all the rest? It wasn't my nature to accept defeat gracefully.

"Chisco!" I yelled inwardly, constricting my throat, not wanting to show my desperation to the others. "Give us a fair chance. Not a miracle, damn it—just a fair chance to make it on our own."

But there was no change. We kept drifting closer and closer to the dreaded reef, bracing ourselves for the inevitable rumble of logs colliding against jagged hunks of coral. We strained our eyes searching for what we didn't want to see: the white-capped lashing of waves against the invisible barrier. The sea became choppier and darker as the moon drifted behind a bank of clouds, and the tension on board mounted with each passing minute.

Then suddenly the wind died down and the waves subsided. We were still drifting westward, but more slowly.

"We're awfully close," said Marc, leaning forward. "I can hear the surf beating against the barrier."

Unable to hear anything myself, I wondered if it was merely his overwrought imagination.

"I can also see the spray," he added. "Over there, to your right. About three hundred yards away."

Sure enough—it was to my right! We had turned somehow. We were drifting south now, with the Great Barrier Reef on our starboard side.

"We're in the current!" I shouted. "We're going to make it."

"I hope so," Marc answered, not entirely convinced. "That reef zigzags a lot. We still have problems."

He was right, of course. The reef had numerous coves and fingerlike projections into the current, none of which would be visible at night. Nevertheless, we were better off than before, even though it was necessary to post a careful four-man watch until sunrise. Shortly before midnight, we got a fairly good wind from the north, which prompted us to hoist our sail again. Every once in a while, as the moon sifted between clouds, we could see the dark cockscomb profile of the reef; then it would disappear again. But as the dawn crept over the eastern horizon the reef emerged in a dazzling display of bright coral, multicolored plants, and sea animals, which we examined through the twin orbits of our binoculars.

By October 28, we were clear of the Great Barrier Reef and moving south, with the Saumarez Reef coming up on our portside. We had a brisk wind and clear blue skies, a perfect day for fishing and sunbathing. Minet was perched on the tip of the cabin roof, watching Marc as he hauled in a wildly flapping dolphin. Patiently retaining his perch as Marc grabbed his knife, he waited until the first blood spurted from the gash, then leaped from the roof in one fluid motion and neatly lapped up the puddle at Marc's feet.

"Minet has developed better manners," observed Marc. "He doesn't slurp any more."

"He's over five months old," I said. "He's maturing."

As we were discussing Minet's progress from greedy kitten to self-assured cat, I heard Normand calling from the crow's nest.

"I see a ship," he yelled. "A big red ship over there."

Looking through the binoculars, I saw an apparently motionless ship. As we drew closer, I noticed what looked like a big gaping hole in its side. Recalling a special mark I had seen on my navigation chart, I unfurled it and found it again. It was a wreck symbol right on the Saumarez Reef. I later learned we were looking at the wreck of an American liberty ship called the *Francis Blair,* which had collided against the reef in 1942. Subsequently, it was used for bombing practice by the RAF, which explained why it was painted red.

Checking my chart again, I said to Gabriel, "If this is the wreck we're looking at, then there should be some huge rocks visible at a hundred twenty degrees southeast."

Sure enough, there they were, two slender rocks sticking up like sharks' fins about three miles away. Beyond them, we could just make out the foamy white line of surf breaking on the reef.

"There's also a white line to our port side," said Normand. "And another one behind the ship."

Suddenly we realized we were in the middle of an immense curving reef, and the wind was blowing us steadily toward the deadly white lines in the distance. Now I could see the rocks below us, about sixty feet down.

"We're headed for trouble," I said to Marc.

"If we escape this one," he replied, "we're damned lucky."

Standing on top of the cabin for a broader view, I held my breath as we approached the first barely submerged coral. Normand was in the crow's nest surveying the area beyond, and Marc and Gabriel were at the *guaras* awaiting instructions, both of them wary and tense.

Passing over that first coral formation, I couldn't help feeling a certain ambivalence, a mixture of cold fear and sheer delight with the incredible spectacle below and around us. The water was a clear emerald green, the convoluted coral shimmering with the bright colors of an artist's palette, and thousands of fish darting in and out among dreamlike underwater plants. It was to be the most beautiful—and the most dangerous—part of our entire voyage.

Angry waves were breaking on two outcrops of coral about half a mile apart. Handling the centerboard *guaras* with the utmost care, we sailed between them and then zigzagged several times to avoid lesser protrusions of the same giant reef, sometimes missing a coral trap by less than three feet. From his perch in the crow's nest, Normand kept warning us that we were still heading for a white line of breakers.

Rushing back and forth between the four *guaras* behind the cabin, I would pull up the starboard boards one moment, then push them down ten seconds later as the raft veered toward a new reef. Then I would scramble to my right to slide the portside *guaras* deeper into the water, turning us away from still another obstacle. And up in front of the cabin, Marc was running back and forth, frantically adjusting the forward *guaras* to coincide with my maneuvers near the stern. It was a kind of split-second acrobatics that must have seemed like madness to Normand.

Then suddenly we found ourselves in a pocket of reefs.

"We're trapped," I said to Marc. "Shall we try to get through?"

"I guess we'll have to."

Having little choice, we steered toward a narrow gap in the churning foam. Marc and I stood on opposite ends of the bow, ignoring the mesmeric beauty of Saumarez, and holding long bamboo poles with which to push away from underwater obstacles. As we came closer, we saw that the gap was barely wide enough for the raft, but it was too late to turn back. Here was the supreme test of *La Balsa's* maneuverability. I shifted the starboard-stern centerboard about six inches to correct a slight list to the left, then held it firm as

191

we started through the gap, catching a spill-over of spray on both sides. Then, when we were halfway through, we heard a loud grinding underneath us, a jolting crunch that knocked us off our feet, as the *guaras* bumped over rocks and coral. Three half-inch ropes that we were trailing for sharks snagged on the coral and snapped. But in a few breathless and terrifying seconds we were over the reef and out into blue water.

Though we had broken three *guaras,* we were safely past the Saumarez Corals. We were on the last lap to Australia.

13

The moment we cleared the Saumarez Reef, Normand started singing at the top of his lungs—the same chorus over and over. We soon joined him with a few *dum de dums* of our own, laughing boisterously at our noisy schoolboy antics, and I realize in retrospect that we were simply relieving the tension that had gripped us when we were crossing the reef. I remember acting the same way after a tough college examination.

The only one who didn't enjoy our foolishness was Minet. He just sat near the bow, twitching his whiskers like a disapproving schoolmaster at noon recess. His amber-green eyes seemed to stare right through us, unblinking and remote.

"What's wrong with Minet?" asked Marc, pausing in the middle of a chorus.

"He feels left out," said Gabriel.

"But he used to meow when Normand sang, don't you remember?"

His sudden silence disturbed us. At first we tried to ignore it, hoping he'd snap out of it. After a while Gabriel and Normand tried to tease him with a crab dangling from a string, then tickled his belly when he refused to play. But nothing worked. He just sat there, scarcely moving a muscle.

Then just before sunset he crept across the forward deck and snuggled into Gabriel's lap, purring softly like a runaway kitten coming home.

That night he kept the watch with me, never leaving my side for three hours, and when Normand relieved me around 3 A.M., Minet immediately climbed into his lap. He had obviously decided to stay up with anyone who was standing watch.

Then it dawned on me that our little cat was afraid to be alone, that even our falling asleep was a kind of abandonment in his eyes. He had somehow sensed we were near journey's end, that we would soon leave *La Balsa,* the only home he had ever known.

On the following afternoon, when Normand harpooned a seven-foot shark, I thought the ensuing commotion would surely stir Minet out of his doldrums, but as the shark thrashed savagely about the deck, Minet sat quietly on the sidelines. Even when Normand slit open the shark's body and reached for its still-throbbing heart, there was no response.

My daily log reflects my continuing concern about our "fifth crew member."

October 30:

We have traveled south about 40 miles today, and we think we've reached the first Australian currents. Everyone is happy except Minet. He's still moping around like a child expecting to be abandoned by divorced parents.

There is no wind today, but we don't mind as long as the current is strong. We certainly don't want a wind from the southeast—that 165-degree wind that has always been our enemy. I've taken our position twice, rechecking the sextant because I can hardly believe we have come down so far.

We've been at sea now five months, two weeks, and one day. We have lost three birds and one cat through illness. The sea has taken six of the seven knives we started with at Guayaquil, and four of the seven kerosene lamps we hung about the raft—mostly to warn other ships of our presence. The cabin has been flooded with water—totally flooded, not merely splashed or washed—five or six times, and we have all been washed overboard at least once. Minet has fallen or been washed into the ocean at least five times.

Our charts and navigation tables have survived the journey, and so has Marc's suit—the same one he took with him on the *Egare II,* the raft that carried him across the Atlantic. Marc likes to have a suit with him when he lands; he has it wrapped neatly in a thick plastic bag. I admire his sartorial pride!

As of today our canasta score is: Marc, 1,617,380; Vital, 1,331,525; Normand 1,268,905; Gabriel, 1,257,350. Though I hesitate to make judgments about comparative ability on the basis of these scores, I think we can assume that older codgers like Marc and me are more patient in such games than youngsters like Gabriel and Normand. Perhaps it's simply a question of experience. *Más sabe el diablo por viejo que por diablo.* (The devil knows more because he's old than because he's the devil.)

November 1:

We're picking up speed. We made sixty-two miles south today. We can safely say we're practically in Australia. Fraser Island is due west of us, although we can't see it yet. Our bad luck seems to be disappearing. I guess we left it behind us on Saumarez Reef.

Again we have a bright phosphorescence. It looks like a sea

of stars beneath *La Balsa*—brighter and more colorful than ever.

November 3:

We need more longitude to the east in case the wind changes and blows us to shore too far north. We want to make sure of getting as far south as Brisbane at least; and if the longitude is favorable enough, we hope to reach Sidney.

Unfortunately, I was wrong in assuming we had left all our bad luck at Saumarez. On the morning of November 3, just after I made my log entry, a bolt of lightning cracked through the leaden gray sky and struck the sea less than a half mile ahead of us, signaling the beginning of a huge storm. Almost immediately we were assaulted by thirty-mile-an-hour winds from 140 degrees southeast. The wrong winds from the wrong direction. Quickly pulling in the sail, we tied everything down as the waves bounced and rocked the raft from bow to stern, flooding the deck with debris from coastal waters and forcing me to hold on to the creaking mast as the waves got higher and meaner.

Marc was nearly swept off the stern but managed to grab hold of a crossbeam at the last moment. Gabriel stayed inside the cabin with the trembling Minet held fast in his arms, mumbling words of comfort whenever a big wave smashed into the bamboo walls.

"Chisco!" I yelled. "This is a dirty trick! You caught us off guard. But you're not going to lick us!"

The only answer I got was the rumbling of wave-upon-wave slashing *La Balsa* with increasing force, the howling wind mounting one attack after another, the logs beneath us straining against the protesting ropes, a dissonant mesh of sounds that seemed like the echo of disaster itself. How long could the ropes hold out against such pressures? Were they, in fact, at the breaking point as Marc had hinted two weeks earlier?

Bending close to the deck, I listened for the snapping sound of ropes tearing apart, but with all the other noises, I couldn't have detected it anyway. Finally, around noon the storm subsided and again the raft had weathered the on-slaught.

Hoping to catch a weather report so as to prepare for any further storms, we pulled out our radio and started fiddling with the receiver. Shortly before 3 P.M. we established contact with Sid Molen in Sydney, who anxiously inquired if we needed anything.

I later learned that Molen, a senior television technician from Pendle Hill, had been in radio contact with Rafael Corcuera at Guadalajara for several months. On October 24, Rafael had asked him to take over the Australian coordination of the raft's communication system, teaching him our click-click question-and-answer technique. Consequently, when Molen called us that afternoon, he had alerted ham operators in Queensland, Victoria, New Guinea, and Lord Howe Island, all of whom were listening and ready to help if necessary but remained silent as Molen commenced a series of questions.

"Do you need urgent assistance?" he asked. "Is anyone sick?"

To which I answered with a click-click (no).

"Do you have enough food and water?"

Long click (yes).

"Would you like a ship to stand by?"

Long click again.

"Do you want to come to the coast?"

An emphatic click-click (NO!)

At this point there was an interruption from Admiral Fernandez in Mexico City, who asked Gus in Aukland to ask us whether the expedition would now end in Brisbane.

I clicked a "yes." We wanted at that time to land at Brisbane, and I wanted a boat to stand by just in case a wind threatened to blow us ashore. After more than eight thousand miles, I didn't want our raft broken apart in a crash landing.

"Can you wait until tomorrow?" asked Sid after a considerable pause.

Long click (yes).

Then I gave him a fairly accurate longitude, responding to questions with the usual clicking. But because of the storm and subsequent cloudy weather, I had not been able to gauge our latitude, and gave him an approximate position based on direction and flow of the current the day before. The southerly current had stopped, however, so the position I reported to Sid (as I discovered the next day) was in fact thirty-seven miles south of us.

Since we were now on a westerly course toward the coast, my mistake caused considerable confusion. On November 4, everyone believed we were much further south, headed for Brisbane, where Captain E. Whish, the Air-Sea Rescue Coordinator, was preparing to meet us.

At about 3:30 A.M., on November 5, Normand saw a light on the distant horizon, a beam of 210 degrees southwest, blinking every seven and a half seconds. Checking my chart with a flashlight, I ascertained that it was the beacon light from Double Island Point, just south of Fraser Island. The notations on the chart said its timing was seven and a half seconds and that it was visible for twenty-four miles.

Now we knew exactly where we were, and I realized that I had misinformed Sid the day before.

When the sun came up three hours later we saw the southern tip of Fraser Island, and I called Marc from the cabin. "There's Australia, *amigo mío*."

Then we all started jumping around the cabin laughing and shouting. Again, everyone was elated except Minet, who sat on his haunches near the stern, quietly staring back at the eastern horizon as if Australia didn't exist.

I got out our radio and started clicking away like an anxious telegrapher, summoning our network of ham operators. Gus, Sid, and a new man named Les Bell from Prosperine were all on the line in less than five minutes. Bell took my position by progressive counting, to which I replied with the appropriate clicks. When the information was relayed to Captain Whish's rescue team, he replied, "That's not possible according to where they were yesterday."

Sid then asked several more questions to confirm our latest position.

"Are you south of Point Danger?"

Click-click (no).

"Are you south of Point Lookout?"

Again the double click for no.

"Are you north of Cape Moreton?"

A long click indicating yes.

"All right, are you northeast of Double Island Point?"

Three long clicks for yes, yes, yes!

"Okay, Vital, we're sending a plane to spot you right away!"

The first plane flew overhead at 9:20 A.M. and dropped an empty beer can near the raft with a piece of paper inside, saying "WELCOME TO AUSTRALIA!"

Then came another plane packed with journalists, followed by several others that kept buzzing over us like friendly bees. Either frightened or resentful (or perhaps both), Minet hid in a corner of the cabin, refusing to join the wild celebration we were staging on deck. After a while I crawled into the cabin and found him huddled in Gabriel's sleeping bag, meowing softly like a heartsick child. I picked him up gently and held him in my lap, stroking his back and trying to console him. Had he somehow realized, with a strange animal prescience, that our "raft family" would soon break up? That we would all go back to our real homes, and that we would never live together again?

Obviously, Minet could only go away with one of us—and, though we hadn't discussed the matter, I guess we all assumed it would be Gabriel. In any case, he would soon lose three of his four parents, and whether or not he would actually miss us once he left the raft, we knew we would miss him. The little cat had given all of us a profound lesson on the art of survival against heavy odds. He had shown great courage and fine spirit. He had survived the disease that killed three parrots and a fellow cat; he had been washed overboard five or six times; he had learned to swim in the shark-infested waters of the mid-Pacific; he had quenched a voracious thirst with the fresh blood of sharks and dolphins; he had shaken himself free from the beak of a kidnapping albatross; he had saved his own life in one of the fiercest storms at sea by clinging tenaciously to the mast with his sharp claws—and he had defied all these dangers with the elan of a soldier of fortune.

There were times, especially in the first few weeks, when I had resented him as a spoiled brat, futilely trying to curb his innate delinquency. But I had inevitably come to

200

respect and to love his great spirit, his piquant charm when the going was tough. Overwhelmed by such feelings, I took Minet outside to join his family, and they all greeted him fondly and invited him to share the lunch Normand had cooked.

As we sat down together, I noticed that Marc was eating with considerable gusto and no longer disdained Normand's amateur cooking by lowering his jaw with every half-chewed mouthful. I also noted that Gabriel was eating hungrily, but quietly, without his usual *craaack* and *raaasp* on the metal spoon. It was the first pleasant meal I had eaten since leaving Guayaquil.

Though Marc and I both had suffered severe indigestion for three months, and I had been ill with a high fever for forty-five days early in the voyage, we were now all in good health. None of us had suffered any serious injury, so fortunately I hadn't needed to use my limited medical and surgical training. We had kept our leg and stomach muscles in tune with gymnastic exercises and some yoga, and there had been work enough for our arms and shoulders, handling the sail and cordage and hauling in fish. Countless games of canasta and Parcheesi, interspersed with long philosophical discussions, had warded off boredom and kept us intellectually alive.

We had also proved that four men can live on a "floating prison" for more than five months without succumbing to the urge to kill. In fact, by carefully adhering to our two rules against personal criticisms and physical contact, we had managed to avoid even a brawl or serious dispute.

Of even greater significance, we had demonstrated that it was possible to navigate a raft with considerable accuracy, that one need not drift with the caprice of winds and currents. We had, in fact, come through some of the most dangerous seas in the world and successfully maneuvered past no fewer than nine treacherous reefs at night. We had also shown that a balsa raft of good female logs retains its buoyancy over long distances. Now at the very end of our voyage, the logs sat only slightly more than one inch deeper in the water than they had in Guayaquil. Had we wanted to sail the raft back to South America, I was sure we could last the distance after tightening the ropes to take up the slack.

The French raft explorer Eric de Bisschop, who died in 1958 after a voyage from Peru to the Cook Islands, believed there had been circular migration from Peru to Polynesia and back again to South America via west-to-east currents. I wanted to show that well-selected balsa logs were capable of covering that distance (a little more than eight thousand miles). Someday I may undertake that round-trip myself. Juan Moricz, the Argentine anthropologist, says that the sea is like the land. It has roads, moving roads, which are the currents. No one knows which travelers used these roads in the distant past, but Moricz believes that Huancavilca Indian rafts may have sailed from the Galapagos Islands to Polynesia. The *Kon-Tiki* proved that a raft was capable of such a journey, and *La Balsa* showed that such a raft was capable of traveling twice that distance—from Ecuador to Polynesia and back again.

The experienced sailors of high cultures of Central and South America knew all about the movement of the sun, moon, and stars, and it's reasonable to assume that they used that knowledge to guide them across the vast ocean. Their use of *guaras* is clear evidence of sophisticated navigation.

Our fourth objective was to gather information about

water and air temperature and atmospheric pressure, which we periodically relayed to the Marine Department of Mexico. We also gathered data about various currents for the Institute of Oceanology at La Jolla, California, revealing that conventional charts were sometimes wrong about the speed and direction of certain currents.

Our final objective was to show that the sea need not be an enemy. I remember reading about the panic of people in lifeboats after the Titanic went down. They were frightened to be cast adrift on the high seas, terrified at the prospect of starving or being eaten alive by sharks, worried about being confined in a small boat with other people. A raft or boat on the high seas is really a small world unto itself. Each man must be responsible for the welfare of the whole group, he must be totally unselfish, ready to help others, to put their lives ahead of his and to give his own if necessary. Survival depends on the total cooperation of *all* men—whether their world is a raft, village, a country, or a planet. The voyage of *La Balsa* had shown that such cooperation is possible and that the sea, for all its immense power, need not be feared as a mortal enemy.

These were my thoughts as we sailed the last few miles to Australia, accompanied by an escort of small planes and scores of pleasure craft. They gave us fruit, candy, and beer, and asked hundreds of questions about the raft. Later that afternoon, five miles off shore, we had a visit from a man named Don Tracey, one of the skippers of the Australian Navy pilot ship *Matthew Flinders,* based at Mooloolaba, about sixty-five miles north of Brisbane. He came on a speedboat called *Capri* and gave us our first official welcome to Australia. But when he saw Minet, he looked concerned.

"You may have a bit of trouble there," he said. "We've got some pretty nasty quarantine regulations on animals, I'm afraid. But we'll see."

Then he offered to tow us the rest of the way, but we politely declined. "We want to go as far as possible on our own," I said. "But perhaps you can tow us at the very end. We don't know this port and we wouldn't want to risk damaging the raft."

"I quite understand, old chap," he answered with a smile. "You let me know when you need me. We'll stay with you from here on."

The area we were headed for is known as the Sunshine Coast, a resort that somehow reminded me of the Costa del Sol on the Mediterranean shores of southern Spain. I was particularly fascinated with the name of its port, Mooloolaba, a musical rolling of full vowels and soft consonants that spoke of mystery and beauty.

It was quite dark when we came into the estuary of the Mooloolaba River, too dark for us to see any dangerous obstacles, so we agreed to let Don Tracey tow us into port with his fine skill and complete knowledge of the night-shrouded bay. We stood at the bow anxiously watching the white-capped spray gushing from the stern of the *Capri*, the backlash creating a slight choppiness that slowed us down. Shortly before midnight we drew near the dock, which we could barely see through the darkness.

Then, suddenly, there was an explosion of light and noise. Sky rockets, Roman candles, blue flares, and all kinds of fireworks shot up from the docks, and hundreds of well-wishers shouted and cheered as *La Balsa* pulled into port:

"WELCOME TO AUSTRALIA!"

14

The tumultuous welcome we received at Mooloolaba soured when two quarantine officers boarded the raft and took Minet away in a metal cage. Tracey had warned us of Australia's strict regulations on the importation of foreign animals, but we hadn't expected their officials to arrive at midnight, less than fifteen minutes after our arrival.

"Let them take her," said Tracey, glancing nervously at Gabriel, whose fists were tightened in anger. "No sense raising a fuss at this hour. We'll talk to the bossman tomorrow morning."

Realizing the quarantine officers were simply carrying out routine orders, we let them take Minet away without protest; but we planned to spring him as soon as possible. With Tracey leading the way, we left the anchored raft and climbed a wooden ladder at the end of the dock, jabbering among ourselves about how good it felt to be on land again. Hundreds of well-wishers lined the dock, stepping back to form a narrow passage for us. Waving back to their welcoming shouts, I started walking through the gap with the snappy military stride I had learned in the Foreign Legion. Then suddenly, before I had taken even three or four steps, my legs buckled. Gabriel and Normand fell in a heap beside me, and Marc wobbled into the arms of two men. The crowd around us gasped in alarm, moving forward in a body to help us. But when they heard us laughing at ourselves, they started clapping and shouting "bravo!"

"Your cheers have made us drunk," I said to those nearest me.

"You're going to feel drunk until you get back your land legs," said Tracey, holding my elbow. "It may be a week before you're steady."

We hadn't touched a steady surface for almost six months, and we were experiencing the punch-drunk syndrome that affects all sailors when they first step on *terra firma*. In fact, ours would be worse because the motions of a small raft are more acute and agitated than those of a large merchant or naval vessel. I remember the slight unsteadiness I had felt when we were on board the gently rocking U.S.S. *Hall,* which seemed as motionless as a football field compared to *La Balsa.*

Yet, in spite of the wobbliness, we somehow managed to enjoy those first few hours on land. Bracing ourselves on the shoulders of several new acquaintances, we shook hands with hundreds of men, women, and children; but we found it almost impossible to autograph the notebooks, slips of paper, menus, and napkins that were shoved into our hands. "I can't stand still," I kept telling them in my heavily accented English.

About an hour after midnight, we had a press conference at the crowded Mooloolaba Yacht Club, feeling less woozy as we sat on solid wooden chairs facing a jumble of microphones and television cameras.

"How do you feel, Captain?"

"Tired and happy."

"Also hungry," added Gabriel, evoking a burst of laughter.

"Were you ever afraid?"

"Quite often," I said. "But I managed to hide it. Mostly from myself."

Some of the questions were confusing because of the language barrier, but the problem of communication was quickly solved by a charming woman named Edith St. Clair-Telford, who spoke excellent Spanish and French. Besides serving as our volunteer interpreter, she immediately adopted us and insisted that we stay at her beautiful estate called Maroochydoore. She spoke of us as *mes enfants* (my children), and we called her *Mama Poule* (mother hen), a name which she herself suggested.

And like a good mother hen, she chased away several journalists and well-wishers who had accompanied us to Maroochydoore. *"Mes enfants* must rest now," she told them firmly. "It's almost four A.M.!"

It was already sunrise when I finally fell asleep. I had stayed awake two hours thinking about Denise and my daughters, Marina and little Denise, wondering if they would still recognize me after an absence of eight months. I had talked to them about an hour after our arrival (Admiral Fernandez had arranged for them to greet me on his ham radio set), and Marina had asked me to bring her a mama kangaroo "with a baby in her pocket." My wife had sounded wonderfully happy and excited, but little Denise seemed subdued and tentative, perhaps confused by the complex dials and knobs on the Admiral's transceiver. Suddenly I felt sad and guilty, a lump rising in my throat as I visualized her standing in front of a cold metal radio apparatus, trying to sound affectionate for a long-absent father she couldn't see, perhaps wondering if the static was not part of my voice. She was, after all, only four years old, and her imagination had always been rather exceptional.

"Did you drown?" she finally asked.

"No, I'm still here, *mi corazón*," I said. "Everyone's fine."

"Is the little kitty still there?" she asked after a short pause.

"Yes, Minet's still with us."

"Bring him home, Daddy," she said with sudden enthusiasm. "And bring Marina a baby kangaroo like the pictures Mama showed us."

I would have promised them the moon wrapped in cellophane, but our conversation was abruptly terminated by shrill static that stabbed my ear drums like an invisible knife. Hoping my daughters hadn't heard the screechy noise on their end of the line, I had said goodbye into the dead microphone and returned to the press conference.

Later on, another local radio ham told me he'd just been contacted by Rafael Corcuera, who wished to congratulate us. Our conversation was lighthearted and friendly, yet I detected a slight edge of sadness in Rafael's voice, a hint of weary resignation that he had tried to mask with sudden spurts of aggressive cheerfulness.

I was still thinking about Rafael when the soft morning

light gradually invaded my bedroom. Turning from the half-shaded window, I faced the opposite wall and closed my tired eyes tight as a fist. I still couldn't sleep. The bed was too stable, the pale blue walls too stationary. After the close confines of our little cabin, this huge beautiful room at Maroochydoore seemed lifeless and empty, impossible to sleep in. I rolled out of bed, and began doing push-ups on the thick blue rug, hoping to tire myself out completely. Finally I managed to fall into a restless stupor that soon transformed itself into a deep sleep.

Gabriel, who had apparently had no difficulty falling asleep, awakened me shortly after nine o'clock. He was wearing a new shirt our hostess had given him and well-pressed trousers.

"We have to get Minet," he said impatiently. "The quarantine office is already open. Normand and Marc are waiting downstairs."

"I'll be ready in fifteen minutes," I said.

With our helpful Mama Poule at our side, we arrived at the waterfront office of the Australian Quarantine Department at ten o'clock. Twenty or thirty news reporters and television cameramen were there ahead of us, apparently hoping to photograph "the cat who had learned to swim among the sharks." Crowding into the gray-walled reception room behind us, they bore witness to a scene that was to make Minet a *cause célèbre* throughout Australia.

"We have come for the cat," I said to a pleasant-faced man behind a black metal desk. "You took it for quarantine last night."

"I'm sorry, sir," he said, nervously eyeing the red light on a TV camera. "We can't let you have her. She's got to stay in quarantine, you know."

"For how long?"

"Well, it's always thirty days, sir. She's got to be checked for communicable diseases. Same as all animals."

"Then what happens?" asked one of the reporters. "After the thirty days?"

The official cleared his throat and shuffled some papers, his worried blue eyes avoiding ours. "I'd rather not say," he said.

"We want to know," I insisted, leaning across the desk.

"There's rules," he mumbled. "I didn't make them."

"What rules?" asked Edith.

"There's regulations that govern all animals that come in."

"But what are they?" she persisted. "How do they apply to the cat these gentlemen brought with them?"

"Well—" he said, with great reluctance. "I'm afraid she's got to be disposed of."

Everyone gasped—even the supposedly calloused newsmen.

"Disposed of!" yelled someone at the rear of the room. "You mean kill her?"

"Well, I wouldn't want to put it that way, sir. It's just the law I'm talking about. It's pretty strict, you know. All ani—"

His voice was drowned in a bedlam of angry protests and snarled threats from all corners of the room. Several police officers from the nearby immigration department rushed in to quiet the uproar, and the quarantine official disappeared into an interior office.

"We won't permit this!" shouted a female reporter. "We'll raise hell with all of you. Watch the headlines!"

"And the telly," said another voice.

Within a few hours the news had spread to every province and town in Australia, the wire services carrying angry articles condemning the Quarantine Department and asking for new laws prohibiting the slaughter of innocent animals. Minet's picture appeared on front pages everywhere, and the evening telecasts carried filmed coverage of our morning encounter at the waterfront. Vehement editorials demanded that the government release "the cat heroine who had survived the toughest sea journey in all recorded history."

Glancing at an eight-column headline, Gabriel observed that the Australian press had altered Minet's sex without benefit of surgery. "He's a female now. They keep referring to him as *her*."

"It's because of his name," I said, reaching for a second serving of a delicious seafood casserole Edith had made for us. "Minet sounds like a feminine name in English. But let's not correct them. I think a female cat arouses more sympathy."

She did indeed. Thousands of letters, mostly from women, poured into the mail pouches of newspapers and government offices, demanding "justice" or pleading for mercy. SAVE MINET . . . FREE THE HEROINE . . . DON'T LET HER DIE . . . MINET MUST LIVE. . . . A veritable blizzard of written protests that no government with any political sensitivity could afford to ignore. Within twenty-four hours several elected officials had asked the administration to reconsider its regulations; and the next day a spokesman for the government publicly announced that the "Minet matter" was under review by higher authorities.

"They're looking for an out," said Edith as she switched to another channel. "They wouldn't dare kill that cat."

Fortunately for everyone concerned, the government was spared further embarrassment by the wife of a sea cap-

211

tain whose ship was about to sail from Brisbane. "I'll adopt Minet," she announced in a telegram to the much-relieved quarantine officials. "She'll find a home on the ship *Sued,* which will leave your country within five days."

Since we would be traveling through Australia, attending receptions in various provinces for two or three weeks, we decided to let her have Minet with the agreement that Gabriel could pick him up at some port along the route of the *Sued.* But when the captain's wife later informed Gabriel that Minet seemed "wonderfully happy" aboard the huge ocean liner, he reluctantly agreed to let him stay.

"That little cat is a born sailor," he subsequently wrote me. "I don't think he could adjust to the desert of Antofogasta. And where would I get him enough shark's blood?"

After our "hero's tour" of the major cities (our hands swollen from too many handshakes, our jaw muscles worn out from continuous smiling), Marc, Normand, Gabriel, and I parted company and returned to our respective homes. But before our departure we had a farewell party on the raft, a rather boozy sentimental affair that lasted until dawn. Lounging on the shredded mat in front of our weather-battered cabin, we talked a lot about Minet and about all the dangers we had overcome, about the great meals Marc had prepared, about the occasional moments of discord, laughing and hugging each with great gusto as we discussed the difficult success of my two rules against touching or criticizing each other.

"I wanted to punch your mouth every time you cleared your throat, Vital," said Gabriel with a smile. "One afternoon—sometime in August—you cleared your throat twenty-nine times in a single hour! I counted them."

212

Then, before I could mention it, Normand spoke up about the way Gabriel had *craacked* and *raasped* on his tiny spoon, "finally forcing me to eat outside the cabin because I couldn't stand it any more."

"I guess I was nervous," explained Gabriel rather sheepishly, tugging a loose banana leaf on the cabin roof. "But I wasn't aware of it. Anyway, I'm glad you didn't criticize me. I would have stopped eating altogether if I'd known how awful it sounded."

Marc grinned and slowly shook his head as he leaned against the cabin wall. "No, that would never happen, Gabriel. Nothing could keep you from eating. I envy you your stomach, my friend—and also your ability to sleep when nobody else could. With that kind of gift, you can survive anything."

Thus praising and forgiving each other, we cemented a friendship that is rare—the profound camaraderie of four men who have traveled far together, who have faced death at the same threshold, thumbing their noses at the gods of chance and somehow jointly managing to survive the worse privations.

My crewmates had become more than brothers to me and I would not forget them—nor the raft, nor Minet, nor the immense track of water we had followed from Guayaquil to Mooloolaba. They were all a part of me and of each other. Leaving Australia on a 707 jet two days later, after arranging to ship *La Balsa* to my hometown in Spain, I looked down at the sparkling waters of the Pacific with affection and awe. Had we really crossed that huge mass of water in a primitive raft? It hardly seemed possible, especially when I saw the maze of deadly reefs along the route we had taken.

Stranger still was my reaction when the stewardess informed me that it would take us twenty-three hours to reach Mexico City.

"Twenty-three hours!" I exclaimed, forgetting we had taken nearly six months to travel a shorter distance. "That's a long time to stay in the same plane. I'll get claustrophobia."

Even with the long stopover in Tahiti, I felt cooped up and virtually imprisoned inside the huge almost empty jet. How I longed for the freedom of *La Balsa,* the nearness of the pulsating water, the comfort of friendly fish trailing behind us, the satisfaction of controlling one's own destiny, something no airline passenger can ever feel.

When we finally landed in Mexico the following day, I almost stumbled on the gangplank rushing off the plane. My wife and children and several friends were waiting for me in the reception area, and there were tears and laughter and warm embraces all around. I thought my wife and daughters were more beautiful than ever as I hugged and kissed them, picking up the little girls in my arms. But our reunion was brief. Denise and I had to board another plane almost immediately. The President of Ecuador, José María Velasco-Ibarra, had invited us to a giant homecoming celebration in Guayaquil.

Within a few hours we were reunited with such friends as Don Cesar Iglesias, Señora Paladines, Joe Megan, and the many Ecuadorians who had given us aid and comfort right from the beginning. There was much joking and reminiscing, with Megan feigning elaborate surprise at the success of the voyage. "You know," he confessed, "I really didn't believe you were anywhere near Australia till I heard it from that American ship. I figured you were holed up on some lava pile in the Galapagos, feeding the cormorants and sending out fake progress reports on that hopeless radio of yours."

"He almost didn't make it to the Galapagos," said Don Cesar, and proceeded to entertain the assembled company with the story of my foolhardy encounter with the poisonous ants of the balsa forest. Señora Paladines wanted to know all about Minet and beamed with an I-told-you-so attitude when I described his various feats of survival. We toasted *La Balsa*, Minet, Megan's radio, and each other, with a special toast to President Velasco, who had cut through all the red tape with the immigration officials on our departure from Guayaquil.

Then we flew back home to Mexico, and the following morning I took my little daughters to an amusement park to celebrate. Dressed in bright-colored new dresses, with saucy beribboned pigtails bouncing off their shoulders, they led me hand-in-hand from the merry-go-round to the scooter to the funhouse and to several refreshment stands in between. But when they asked me to take them on the roller coaster, known as *la Montaña Rusa,* or the Russian Mountain, I balked.

"It's too dangerous," I said, a queasy sensation gripping my stomach as a coaster full of screaming, wide-eyed teenagers came roaring down the nearly vertical track.

"Mama takes us," said Marina, squeezing my thumb in her tiny hand.

"All the time," added Denise. "Mama likes the roller coaster."

"She must be crazy," I said under my breath. "Only a fool would get on one of those death traps."

"What did you say, Papa?" asked Denise.

"Nothing," I said. "I was just thinking that we ought to take another ride on the merry-go-round."

They followed me without protest, but I distinctly heard Marina whisper to her sister, "I think Daddy's afraid."

Realizing they were too young to understand the difference between rational and irrational risks (roller coasters clearly belonging to the latter category), I bribed them into silence with popcorn and cotton candy and reserved the lecture for my wife, who had just arrived to join us. But Denise simply smiled at my masterful distinction between the calculated risks of a raft on the high seas and the uncontrollable dangers of a roller coaster.

"There's nothing wrong with being afraid of roller coasters, Vital," she said, missing my point entirely. "Everyone has to be afraid of something. I once heard that Manolete was afraid of cats."

Knowing it was useless to defend my position against such intransigence, I led them off to the "caterpillar crawl," mumbling something about the irrationality of the female mind.

The next day I had to leave them again briefly. I had arranged a quick round-trip flight to Guadalajara to visit a friend I had never met personally, Rafael Corcuera, who had followed us so assiduously on his ham radio set. Hoping to surprise him, I had decided not to call him in advance. But when his wife answered the door and I gave her my name, her expression told me something tragic had happened.

"Rafael is dead," she said in a hushed voice, leading me into their modestly furnished living room. "He died just after you finished your voyage. He had been awfully sick for a long time, but he wouldn't let himself die until you had reached Australia."

She paused, touched her graying hair with trembling fingers, and drew a deep breath, tears brimming in her dark brown eyes. "Your wonderful voyage kept him alive. He seemed to be sailing with you, charting your progress day by day on a huge map. He kept worrying about all of you, about your water supplies and about the terrible storms near Samoa. And when he heard of your emergency—when you were almost starving—he couldn't sleep for forty-eight hours."

"He was very kind to us," I said, not wanting her to know that the "emergency" was simply a misunderstanding caused by our faulty radio transmitter.

"We finally moved his bed to the basement where his radio was," she continued. "He was too weak to climb up and down the stairs. So we converted the basement into a radio station and bedroom, and he listened to every broadcast from all the ham operators in the South Pacific. He also told them to listen for any reports from your raft. Oh, how he worried about—as if you were his own children. He would often stare at the map, when your radio went dead, mumbling, 'Where are my sons?' "

Señora Corcuera took me down to the well-kept, freshly painted basement and showed me the log he had kept and the much-marked maps he had used to chart our course, and I felt a mingling of pride and sadness when I noticed how his writing had grown fainter toward the end.

"We loved your husband," I said, looking at the neatly folded covers on his bed. "And we always felt his presence. You might say he was the fifth man on *La Balsa*."   .

"Rafael would have been proud to hear you say that," she said in a soft whisper. "And I'm grateful that you kept him alive as long as you did."

Flying back to Mexico City that evening, I was overwhelmed with gratitude for friends like Rafael Corcuera and for the many unseen strangers who had accompanied us by radio all the way to Mooloolaba.

Sensing that I was still somewhat depressed by my visit to Corcuera's, my wife tried to postpone a large party that had been planned for me by our old friends Norma and Carlos Fink. But when she heard that all our friends would be there, anxiously waiting to see us, we both decided it would be best to go. And I was glad we did. Norma and Carlos had gone to great lengths in preparing for our arrival. It was a marvelous gathering of raft *aficionados* who had supported me from the very outset. Curiously, most of them were doctors who had never before been involved in any aspect of navigation. Our host, Dr. Fink, was a noted cardiovascular surgeon; his good friend, Dr. Ezequiel Alvarez Tostado, a fine gastroenterologist. It was the latter who informed me that the symptoms I had suffered during my forty-five-day illness on *La Balsa* clearly showed that I'd been infected by the same disease that killed our three parrots and the older cat, a lung infection akin to psittacosis. "You're lucky to be alive," he told me.

Two other doctors, Carlos Gomez Medina and Petry Choly, confirmed Dr. Tostado's diagnosis, but my old friend and mentor, Admiral Samuel Fernandez, assured them that "the only thing that can kill Vital Alsar is boredom or shark fever."

There was little time for boredom. The following week the Spanish government was giving an elaborate reception at General Francisco Franco's ornate palace, and I debated whether or not to shave off my shaggy beard. Finally I told Denise, "I guess I'd better not. If I show up in Madrid without my pirate's beard, they'll mistake me for a shoe clerk or a bookkeeper."

I did, however, don my best dark suit and conservative gray tie. It was a pleasant ceremony, and I was given a beautiful bronze medallion. But for all the splendor of the occasion, I couldn't help feeling a certain sympathy for General Franco. Here he was, surrounded by everything money can buy—exquisite tapestries, gleaming marble floors, oriental carpets, finely carved mahogany furniture, gold ashtrays, Etruscan vases, red velvet drapes from floor to ceiling, and discreet ever-ready servants to answer his slightest need. Yet it all seemed like a gilded prison. He had no free access to that world that is most real to me. He could not take a solitary walk down a tree-lined avenue, or window-shop along the Prado, or eat in an ordinary public restaurant in one of those marvelous gypsy *tascas* on the Plaza Mayor. Like any other head of state, he had to be escorted everywhere by a bodyguard, having long ago sacrificed that precious privacy which even the most humble citizen enjoys.

"It must be wonderful to sail on a raft," he said to me on that occasion. "How nice it would be to get away from all the mundane problems of this world."

Had it been possible for him to use it, I would have given him *La Balsa* there and then. Instead we compromised, and with his financial assistance, we established a special sailor's museum in Santander, where *La Balsa* can remain on permanent display. Perhaps it will encourage someone else to take up the challenge of the sea—as the Huancavilcas did—and sail freely toward the western sun.